"The Answer is NO"

D0683959

"The Answer is NO"

Saying it and sticking to it

Cynthia Whitham, MSW

Illustrations by Barry Wetmore

Perspective Publishing

Los Angeles

Copyright © 1994 by Cynthia Whitham
Illustrations copyright © 1994 by Barry Wetmore
All Rights Reserved.

Library of Congress Catalog Card Number 93-087726
ISBN 0-9622036-4-5

Published by Perspective Publishing, Inc., 50 S. DeLacey Ave. Suite 201,
Pasadena, CA 91105, (818) 440-9635

Additional copies of this book may be ordered by calling toll free
1-800-992-6657

Publisher's Cataloging-in-Publication Data

Whitham, Cynthia
    "The answer is NO": saying it and sticking to it/Cynthia
Whitham
      p. cm.
      Includes index
      ISBN 0-9622036-4-5
      1. Discipline of children. 2. Parenting. 3. Parent and child.
I. Title.

HQ770.4.W45 1994   649.6'4
                                                        QBI94-19

Illustrations by Barry Wetmore
Back cover photo by Frank Bates
Printed in the United States of America
Second Printing: 1995

Acknowledgment

I want to thank my publisher Linda Pillsbury, who said to me after my first book, *Win the Whining War* came out, "How about a follow-up—I'm thinking of the title, *'The Answer is NO.'*" I liked it fine. I couldn't hope for a better work/friendship than ours. Here's a When/Then for you, Linda: you keep dreaming up great titles and I'll keep writing books.

Many thanks to my clients and friends who continuously supply me with stories and anecdotes of family troubles and solutions. Keep those kids and conflicts coming.

Thanks, too, to friends and colleagues who took time from busy schedules and lives to read the manuscript and give me feedback: Della Bahan, Dave Bice, Tim and Eileen Bice, Valerie Cummings, Ph.D, Lesley Dewing, Laurel Hitchcock, Susan and Ron Lapekas, Suzanne Levanas, LCSW, Glenn Noreen, and Patrice Yasuda, Ph. D.

Thanks and love and everything to dear, dear friends Masha, Della, Barb, and Sally. What would I do without you? Aren't we overdue for a GNO or two?

All my love to my kids Miranda McLeod and Kyle McLeod. You make it so easy to be a mom.

Contents

Why to Use This Book

Do you have trouble saying "no" to your kids? Do you feel guilty, have trouble being consistent, work at cross purposes with your partner, or tend to run out of problem-solving ideas in the heat of conflict? *"The Answer is NO": Saying it and sticking to it* is a book that will help you say "no" effectively. Each family has different standards. One finds sweets intolerable, another can't bear nagging in stores. One finds TV viewing is out of hand, while another wants a reasonable bedtime. In this book I present solutions to twenty-six of the most challenging situations parents raise at my lectures, workshops, or in my practice as a clinical social worker at UCLA's Parent Training Program.

"The Answer is NO" gives you permission. It not only tells you it is okay to set limits, but insists that children need limits to thrive. When parents provide a consistent structure, clear expectations, and predictable responses and consequences, children are more able to grow into healthy, happy, responsible, and socially agreeable adults.

Think about the times when a child might need his parents to say "no": when he demands a toy that little brother has, insists on playing checkers when a visiting friend would like to play ball, or wants to sleep in his parents' bed when they want to sleep alone. When parents say "no," children begin to learn about the rights of siblings, parents, and friends. They learn to look at life through the eyes of others, the first step in becoming empathetic.

Children also need limits on things or experiences that are just not good for them, such as too many sweets, long hours of TV, or premature dating. We know that saying "no" is what's best, but our kids wear us down and wear us out by arguing and begging. Giving in to nagging or tantrums is very detrimental. Not only have we gone against our better judgment, but also we have given them a dangerous message: if you make a big enough fuss, you'll get want you want eventually. Picture your kids entering their adult life with badgering as one of their primary social skills.

I find that parents' biggest battles occur when they are ambivalent about a behavior and have conflicting values or opinions about it. They want help with a problem, suspect limits are in order, but are torn. They want to be friends with their children, not adversaries. They don't want to have a knee-jerk "no" response to every request. They don't want to be "because I said so" parents. Many find themselves giving in to requests, desires, and demands more than they would like (and more than may be good for their child) or presenting a variety of choices when they really need to take charge.

"The Answer is NO" will help you with that ambivalence by giving you a chance to weigh your values, consider your child's needs, and listen to her feelings. By thinking it over, you then can proceed to establish clear expectations about the behavior and be prepared to address the conflicts that may result.

How to Use This Book

This is not a book you need to read cover-to-cover. Simply turn to the chapter about the problem of your choice and find help saying "no," meaning "no," and sticking to your "no."

If you have already read the companion book, *Win the Whining War and Other Skirmishes: A family peace plan,* many of the techniques will be familiar. *Win the Whining War and Other Skirmishes* provides a step-by-step guide to increasing cooperation and reducing conflict with children two to twelve years old. *"The Answer is NO"* helps you apply the techniques to the specific situations that are causing you trouble. Both books are clear, straightforward, and no-nonsense. I want you to be able to use them easily.

In each chapter I give a three-part approach for handling a specific area of conflict with your child:

1. THINKING IT OVER: A short discussion about the problem situation and the dilemma it offers parents.

2. HOW TO GET...: A hands-on strategy for getting the behavior you want and preventing problems from arising.

3. SAYING NO and STICKING TO IT: What to do if you and your child have already entered The Conflict Zone (you said "no" and it's not working).

Tools such as Time-Out and Warning are capitalized, and you will find further explanations of each tool and technique in the Glossary. Use the Index for finding more examples of how a specific technique might be applied. Examples of dialogue that you can try are printed in italics.

I encourage you to get a good source book on child development. Read about your child's age and what is reasonable to expect of her at that stage. Learn the responsibilities she can handle and the amount of independence she needs. This reading will help you understand her developmental "tasks," where she is going, and what help she needs to get there.

I believe that all adults in the home need to work together to change a child's behavior. I have used the term partner to refer to your spouse, your ex-spouse, your live-in companion, or any adult who participates in raising your child.

Most of the behaviors can be applied to either girls or boys, although I do think adolescent behaviors start earlier for girls than for boys. Rather than use the cumbersome "his/her" or "their," I have more or less alternated "he" and "she" chapters and examples. I have done the same with referring to doctors, teachers, and so on, and hope that everyone feels included.

If, after reading *"The Answer is NO": Saying it and sticking to it*, the problem situations do not improve, that is, you've done your best at sticking to your "no" but your child is into Major Badgering or outright defying your final decisions, seek professional help from a licensed mental health professional who specializes in behavioral parent training.

Always No

There are some things in life that are not negotiable. If you can think of any situation in which you'd tolerate biting, lying, fighting in the car, or being monstrous in company, this book is not for you. Get a refund.

1
Biting

THE PROBLEM:

Your child bites. Not just you (you could handle that, possibly), but also her toddling buddies at day care. You want help, now.

THINKING IT OVER:

No dilemma here. Your kid's clearly the offending party. And you know the rules: no matter how much you are taunted, teased, or lorded over in the sand box, biting is the Number One No-No.

You hear that some children bite because they are not quite verbal enough to express their frustration and anger in words. If a toddler's toy is snatched away by another, she does not have the social skills to say, "You took my truck. That makes me angry. Give it back now." If she is being bullied by a more savvy child, who taunts her when no one is looking, she will strike out in defense without thinking about alternatives.

As your child matures your goal will be to teach her to express her angry feelings by "using her words," assert herself in a non-aggressive way, and get help from teachers and parents if she needs it. She will also need to learn "you can't always get what you want" exactly when you want it. But while her social skills are developing, you need clear, immediate consequences for biting.

KEEPING "TEETH TO SELF":

1 Give your child plenty of opportunity to run, climb, jump, and engage in strenuous play. This may help decrease her excess energy or tension.

2 If your child begins to be aggressive in her play, invite just one child over for a short play date. You may need to supervise their play and intervene by distracting or redirecting them.

3 Praise your child when she plays well with others, shares toys, is helpful to another, asserts herself with words rather than getting physical, or has a play date without incident:

> *You did a good job playing with Gretchen today. I liked*
> *how you shared the blocks and the horses.*

4 Watch yourself. How do you handle frustration? If you fly off the handle, you are teaching your child to do the same.

SAYING NO and STICKING TO IT:

1 When your nursing baby bites you, try not to scream. What fun it is to get mom to open her eyes wide, gasp, and yelp, *"Oh, you little bum, you bit me!"* Be careful not to give her the reward of your attention by laughing (it won't be cute long) or yelling at her. Just avert your eyes and carefully disengage yourself.

2 When your toddling baby bites, look her in the eye and give the firm Command, *"No biting."* This may be enough to stop her.

3 Establish clear Consequences for biting. Before going to play at the park or a friend's house, give the Warning:

> *If you bite, we will leave.*

If she bites, gather your things and go.

4 Never bite back. Biting back does not give a toddler the insight, "Gee, it hurts when Mom bites me. I guess I shouldn't do that to others." In her frustration and fury, your child is not going to get any major insight into the cause-effect relationship between biting and another's pain, believe me.

5   When your child bites at home, give her a Time-Out:

- Pick a place for Time-Out, such as a chair facing a corner, where she is isolated but where you can keep an eye on her. For a child of two you may use her crib or playpen.

- Pick a time limit for Time-Out. For a toddler, forty-five seconds can be plenty.

- Use a kitchen timer so you aren't the time-keeper.

- As soon as she bites, say, *"No biting. Take a Time-Out in this chair. When the timer rings your Time-Out is over."*

- Turn away from your child and go about your business. Do not talk to her, look at her, or touch her. Ignore when your child tries to distract you by falling off her chair, crying, making noises, or asking when Time-Out will be over.

- When the timer rings, say simply and calmly, *"Your Time-Out is over. You may leave the chair."*

6   DO NOT cuddle or soothe your child if she cries during or after Time-Out. This will completely undermine the effectiveness.

A family came to see me with the dilemma that two-year-old Cecily had been kicked out of nursery school for biting, drawing blood, seven times in one week. Both parents and school teachers were using Time-Out, they claimed.

I found that at home Mom ended Time-Out by picking up Cecily and comforting her. I instructed the parents to end Time-Out differently. They were to announce, *"Your Time-Out is over,"* lift her out of the crib, and gently place her on the floor. If Cecily grabbed her mom's legs and clothing, Mom was to turn away and do some activity, such as rinsing dishes or straightening the contents of a drawer. She was to ignore fussing and clutching, but if Cecily began any remotely acceptable behavior, she could respond to her. Within a week, the biting stopped.

7 Don't mix giving a lesson and giving a Consequence. Parents often want to give their children explanations about why biting is bad and how it has hurt the other child. They want to tell her about other ways to express her anger. At the moment of conflict, however, your child is too angry or embarrassed to be able to absorb a social lesson. She will be more receptive during a quiet pre-bedtime talk, when she is calm.

You may find it helpful to draw from the extensive array of books on the market designed to teach children about feelings and how to handle them. Even more helpful might be to give her specific things to do or say instead of biting. Role-play what your child should do (walk away) or say ("I don't like that!") if little Alfred should call her "Poo-poo head" again.

8 If your child is biting at school or child care, make certain teachers and child care workers are using Time-Out correctly.

In the above example, Time-Out at Cecily's school meant going to the director's office. The director talked to her about how biting hurts and that when she's mad she has to use her words.

The problem was not the message, but that the director was rewarding Cecily with attention, when she should have had none. Children will bite or hit more if the "punishment" of Time-Out is, in actuality, the privilege of a private audience with the school's director.

If the school staff is unwilling to use Time-Out at all or insists on using it incorrectly—maintaining that their methods are successful with other children who misbehave—you may have to remove your child from that school. It does not matter what has worked with other children, if it does not work with your child. Luckily Time-Out, used correctly, is a method that works consistently when other methods fail.

2
Car Fighting

THE PROBLEM:

Your children squabble, bicker, tease, mimic each other ("Mom! He's copying me!"), complain, poke, scream, make faces, fight over games, fight over the front seat. You want to be delivered from fighting children at least for the remainder of the trip! Is that really so much to ask?

THINKING IT OVER:

What's there to think over? Nothing. You are in the clear on this one. You have every right in the world to have a reasonably quiet drive as you ferry your children from point A to point B. Journeys of any length can elicit such helpful remarks as, "How long is this going to take?" "This is boring!" and the ever-popular "Are we there yet?" Soon they are relieving their boredom by torturing each other and you.

I have no doubt that before the baby-boomers' baby boom is over, the roll-down glass partition separating the front and back seat (which disappeared in the fifties) will return. But until then, read on for some sanity saving tips.

HOW TO HAVE CONFLICT FREE (okay, okay, conflict-reduced) CAR TRIPS:

1 Praise your kids for any terrific car behavior as soon as it occurs. Particularly praise if they are exhibiting patience or are getting along.

2 Bring travel games in the car. There are nifty check-off pads you can buy in bookstores which keep small eyes searching for signs, landmarks, cars, bridges, and so forth. Stash away some travel-only toys, such as a small chalk board and chalk for tic-tac-toe, a portable video game, or an audio cassette player with earphones. Some kids are able to read in the car; bring plenty of books for those traffic jams or the "let's pull over and look at the map" stops.

3 Bring snacks and drinks along for longer trips. Always carry water. Some parents keep a few non-perishables in the glove compartment like nuts, raisins, or crackers for the ride home after school or daycare.

4 Plan frequent rest stops for long distance travel. They can be short, just a chance to stretch legs, breathe a little air, and look at the scenery. If you are on a trip of several hours, don't just focus on getting there as quickly as possible. You might break up the day with a little side visit to a museum or other attraction.

5 Make a deal. On a four-hour trip to a beach vacation, I gave my kids the following choice:
*We can drive straight there—with one or two shorts stops
for food, gas and going to the bathroom—and be there
before dark, so you guys can swim; or, we can have lots of
stops and get there after dark. It's your choice, but if you
choose driving straight, you'll need to be very patient and
not fight with each other.*

My kids chose to drive directly, and, with a couple of Reminders, did not squabble. We arrived in time for a swim before the sun went down. Who'd have guessed?

If they hadn't come to an agreement, I would have made the decision for them or flipped a coin.

6 Allow your kids to vent their frustration in direct, non-whiny ways ("using their words"). If they say with a sigh, "It's taking forever to get there," respond by saying, *"Yes, it is a long drive. You guys are being very patient. Thanks."* If the same complaint comes out whiny, shrill or nasty, just ignore the remark.

7 Spring a little surprise on them for terrific behavior. Although I do not recommend using food rewards as a regular incentive, a stop for ice cream in the middle of a long, hot trip should inspire even more cooperation.

8 A note on radio usage: I'm a bit of a dictator when it comes to using the radio. I tend to think of the radio as something to help the driver. (I mean, look where they place the controls!)

Parents can nurture "consensus" by teaching their children early to appreciate their personal favorite recording artists. I gave my kids "valuable prizes" for being able to identify a Smokey Robinson, Beatles, Aretha, James Brown or Righteous Brothers tune from my oldie station. Sure, they'd have prefered a pop station, but they settled for singing along with Mom and clearing her out of meter money for accurate guesses.

If you want to be democratic about using the radio, fine. Alternate stations or audio tapes. On the way, sister can have her rap and on the way back, brother can have his rock. The next trip it's your turn. Or invest in radio or tape headsets. You can all bop down the highway, each hearing a different drummer.

SAYING NO and STICKING TO IT:

1 If, in spite of great vibes emanating from the driver's seat, the ruckus starts, don't beg, plead, or threaten. Simply state an appropriate Command:

Keep your hands to yourself.

Keep your voices down, please.

If you cannot play that game without fussing, I'm going to put it away for fifteen minutes.

2 If they comply, praise them immediately. Continue to praise periodically.

Thanks, kids, for keeping your hands to yourself.

It's very quiet back there, I appreciate your keeping your voices down.

That game sounds like a lot of fun—you guys have been at it for ages.

Consider a small reward or privilege to celebrate a peaceful remainder of the trip.

3 If they continue to battle, your next Command can be non-verbal. Simply and calmly, pull to the side of the road, or take the next off-ramp of the highway, turn off the ignition, and wait. When your children quiet, simply say, *"Thank you."* Start the car and go.

If they demand you drive or explain yourself, say, *"When you can keep your hands to yourself, then I will drive."* At that point they usually will quiet down and you can say, *"Thank you"* and turn on the motor.

By the way, if your young child takes off his seatbelt or climbs out of his carseat, the side of the road tactic works for the younger set as well.

It's a good idea to leave five to ten minutes early when you're planning on using this excellent ignoring technique.

4 You may need to do the starting-stopping bit more than once to show you mean business. Again, calmly pull to the side of the road. Do not show your anger or frustration. When the kids have ceased disturbing each other, thank them and continue to drive.

5 You may not have time to stop the car. If they are complaining to you about each other, simple ignore it. Or announce, *"You two need to work it out yourselves."* If squabbling escalates, your next step is to give a Warning of a Consequence. To be effective the Consequence must have meaning for the child and you must have control over it.

A mother at one of my lectures said she uses this warning with success, *"If you can't keep quiet, kids, I'll sing show tunes."* Other possible Warnings of Consequences are:

Joey, keep your hands to yourself or you'll have to sit up front with me.

Lower your voices or you will go to bed fifteen minutes early tonight.

If you use bad language again, you will be fined fifty cents a word.

Stop the teasing or we will go back home. (only if you're willing to do it)

Whoever hits will have to unpack the car all by himself.

Be sure to follow through with giving the Consequence if they earn it.

6 If you have chronic in-car fighting and drives for family outings are inspiring suicidal thoughts, then give the Trial Run a go:

* Plan an outing that requires a half-hour drive. Make it an activity the kids like to do (miniature golf, bowling, hiking, going to the beach), but that doesn't require any

advance purchase of tickets.

- Before you get in the car, sit down with your kids, make eye contact with each of them, and clearly spell out three rules of behavior, such as:
  No teasing each other, and that means no copying, making faces, or calling names."

  Keep your hands, feet and all other body parts to yourself.

  Use talking voices only, no screaming.

- Give a Warning of Consequence: *"If any one of you breaks any one of the rules, we turn around and head home."*

- Make sure they understand the rules and the Consequence.

- Be prepared to turn around. In fact, have a tentative sitter lined up, so if you have to bring the kids home you can take yourself to the movies!

- Start driving. Praise them after a few minutes if they cooperate with the rules.

- If they break a rule, don't say a word. Turn around the car and head home. Ignore all protests. When you get home, provide no extra fun. Let them help themselves to lunch: *"There's fruit, cheese, peanut butter and eggs in the fridge, guys."* Take a nice hot bath or read a good book.

I don't think you will have much car fighting in the future!

3
Lying

THE PROBLEM:

Your child stretches the truth, avoids the truth, or out-and-out lies to you. You could tolerate almost any other behavior, but not lying. You simply insist that your child be honest.

THINKING IT OVER:

There is not much to think over about lying. Lying is truly the behavior which drives all parents to distraction.

Lying starts simply enough. Children at an early age don't easily differentiate fantasy from reality. Their truth and their wishes are all entangled. It is common for a little child to describe something she yearns for as something she already has, or something she wishes to do as something she's already done.

Later on, children use lying to keep from getting into trouble. They can have cookie crumbs all over their faces and claim with quite believable earnestness, "I didn't take any cookies." They hope, by saying "I didn't do it," to be saved from punishment. They hope so much, they sometimes begin to believe in their own innocence.

Lying is not only a bad strategy (the truth is usually found out), but it is a very unacceptable behavior in most life settings. Read further for a few ideas on how to curtail lying.

HOW TO GET NOTHING BUT THE TRUTH:

1 Model taking responsibility. Set an example of someone who is not afraid to tell the truth and face the consequences.

If someone hollers from the kitchen, "Who finished the milk? I was going to use it to make brownies," it's very good for a child to hear the other parent call in response, *"Sorry, honey, I didn't realize you needed it. I'll be happy to go get more."*

2 Model being honest. If someone calls on the telephone and you don't want to speak to him, don't ask your child or spouse to lie. Instead have your child say, *"My dad is busy and can't come to the phone now. May he call you back?"*

3 Don't lie to your children. If they ask you something which you cannot tell the truth about (something they would not understand or would confuse or scare them), say something like, *"That's something which your mother and I need to keep private."*

4 If you are worried about your pre-schooler's fantasy wishes (although I don't know that you need be) you may re-frame her fantasies to realities: *"You don't have a horse, but you sure would like to have a horse, wouldn't you?"* You can further help by teaching the difference between "pretend" and "real."

5 Use fables and fairy tales to impress upon your child the importance of truth. Both *Pinnocchio* and *The Boy Who Cried Wolf* present clear consequences for lying.

6 Reward the truth. If a child comes forward and tells you about something bad that happened (he broke something, lost something, got in trouble at school), take the opportunity to praise him.

I am not happy that you had to be benched today, but I
appreciate that you were brave and came to tell me.

Your child will not be so afraid of telling the truth, because you have handled it so well!

7 Since it is possible your child might lie to get attention, don't take the good stuff for granted. Show interest in the little things and praise the day-to-day successes. Take some time each night to sit down, unwind, and talk honestly with your child about his day.

SAYING NO and STICKING TO IT:

1 Don't interrogate. If you are pretty sure your child has done something you don't like, make a statement to the child, rather than badger him with questions. When a child knows he is in trouble, he is already upset and worried. He will be tempted to lie to avoid punishment. (Have you ever been stopped by a police officer for a traffic violation? Did you try to talk your way out of it? Did you readily admit you were at fault?)

Rather than say, "Did you break Mr. Hill's window when you were playing ball?" say instead, *"You guys broke Mr. Hill's window when you were playing ball. Come on, let's get Jeff and Frank and go apologize to Mr. Hill."*

2 If you find your child has lied, give a Consequence. A Consequence is the loss of a privilege—

Which has meaning for the child

Over which you have control

Which you are willing to take away, and

Which is minimal in duration.

If there is a connection between the offense and the Consequence, that is ideal. For example, if he lies about playing outside the boundaries you have set, the Consequence might be playing inside that afternoon.

3 Since kids lie to avoid punishment, set up a rule that if you lie to cover up a misbehavior and are caught, there will be two Consequences, one for the misbehavior and one for the cover-up.

4 If your child insists he didn't do it, but you're pretty sure he did, avoid the battle if you possibly can. He may insist so fervently that he comes to believe in his innocence. I would rather see a parent err in the wrong direction for a child who has a chronic problem with lying. You might say, *"Perhaps you weren't playing ball exactly when Mr. Hill's window was broken, but his window was broken yesterday and you and the guys were playing ball yesterday. If I find I have made a mistake, I will apologize. For now, though, we need to go over and fix Mr. Hill's window."*

5 A child who lies may, like in the *Boy Who Cried Wolf*, find that the one time he tells the truth no one will believe him. Explain that although you know he is working hard to tell the truth, because he has lied in the past, not everyone is willing to trust him yet. A little more time will be needed.

4
Rotten Restaurant Behavior

THE PROBLEM:

You're out to eat at a restaurant with family or friends. Your child refuses to sit where he needs to or eat what he's ordered. He demands a soft drink when your rule is water, milk, or juice, or continually interrupts adult conversation although there are other kids at the table. He demands that you go to a different restaurant or spends half the evening sitting on your lap. You'd like to enjoy your meal and the company, not wish you'd hired a sitter and left the youngster at home.

THINKING IT OVER:

We're talking about more than kicking under the table or sloppy table manners here. We're talking about what seems to be a plot to ruin your evening. You are with your family, relatives, or friends. Maybe this outing is a rare treat. Special occasion or not, you don't want your kid to ruin it for everyone.

The specific behavior is unpredictable. He doesn't want to order from the kid's menu (which he normally loves and which your pocketbook requires). When the food arrives it doesn't meet his suddenly higher standards. The macaroni and cheese is too cheesy, the spaghetti sauce has mushrooms in it, or the burrito has the wrong kind of beans. He's just in a huff and picks a time when you are most vulnerable, out with family or friends.

You try to placate him, but to no avail. If you give in to his ruining the seating plan, he'll skirmish with you over the menu. If you give in to his food demands, he'll battle over dessert. If you give in to the dessert demands, he'll interrupt your conversation. You try to excuse the behavior; your little guy hasn't seen you all day or he's over-tired. He's just gotten over a cold or maybe he's coming down with one. It's long past his dinner time and he's starving. But in truth you all are tired and you all are hungry and he's the only one out of control.

Let me reassure you: you have a right to a non-stress meal with friends and family. You have a right to have your child behave well in public. He needs your help to develop better restaurant habits, so use the following plan.

HOW TO HAVE A PLEASANT RESTAURANT MEAL WITH CHILDREN:

1 From early on, expect good behavior from your child. Establish clear restaurant rules: eat with utensils, chew with mouth closed, talk only when mouth is empty, keep hands and feet to self, ask for things to be passed rather than reaching, say "please" and "thank you," be courteous to restaurant staff, accept the limitations of the menu or pocketbook, and (yes, I'm afraid we have to spell this one out too) no loud burping or other bodily noises.

2 Practice the rules at fast food and family style restaurants. On special occasions go to more formal restaurants where children are welcome. Praise or even reward terrific behavior whenever you see it. If your child breaks the rules, give a Consequence. Consequences can range from your child leaving the table for a Time-Out to your taking your child home from the restaurant (more on that later).

3 Establish similar expectations for your child when visiting friends' homes for barbecues, potlucks, or sit-down dinners. You can practice giving Consequences among friends, where you will be supported in your efforts.

4 If your child tends to act up when you're out, assess the situation. Is he tired? Is he hungry? Does he want your attention because you've been at work all day? Are you with kids he can't stand?

From your assessment, decide how to avoid the situation next time:

- Plan a nap for the child who may get sleepy early.

- Give the hungry child a snack in the car.

- Invite a buddy of his to join you for dinner.

- Suggest a more workable seating plan (dinner sitting beside you and dessert beside the kids).

5 Bring along quiet instruments of distraction to the restaurant: coloring book and crayons, a pack of cards, a small plastic box with a few play figures, picture or reading books, or small, portable travel games.

6 Tune in to your child's developmental needs. For instance, with the four-year-old, routine is your best friend. Have a family restaurant which you go to on a regular basis. Sit in the same booth, pray for the same friendly waitress, and tip heavily for her remembering to greet your little guy with crackers, crayons, or neon cherries.

Think picnic and potluck if your child is at one of the notorious stages when it's expected that he'll be impossible in public.

7 If your child usually cooperates well on outings, but tends to have trouble with a particular family, relative, or setting, I don't think it hurts to use a little Mirroring to let him know you understand his discomfort:

> *I know that it's hard for you when we eat out with the Jones's—and that Wendy sticks to you like glue and you hate that.*

You might go further and ask how he can make things go more smoothly at dinner:

> *What do you think I could do to help things out? How about if you and Simon sit next to each other and Wendy sits next to her dad?*

8 Again, with a child who basically is cooperative, but needs a little inspiration to get through a challenging occasion, use an offer of a When/Then Deal:

> *If you can do a great job going out to brunch with the Jones's this morning, this afternoon you can have a playdate with any friend you choose.*

9 Give a Reminder; all kids need them. In the car on the way to the restaurant, announce the two or three regular rules, and give a brief Reminder of them again as you enter the restaurant. In a few minutes, before your child has had time to do anything but be terrific (I hope), praise your child for cooperating with the rules. Continue to praise good behavior throughout the meal.

10 Use the Trial Run to establish that you mean business out at restaurants. Trial Runs are low-stress for you, because you know it's staged, but have all the benefit of the Real Thing for kids. The steps for a Restaurant Trial Run are:

- Pick an inexpensive restaurant (fast food is ideal) which your kids like. You eat before hand.

- Announce the rules for the outing, such as:
  Keep your feet to yourself (no kicking under the table).
  Stay seated until everyone is finished.
  No begging for extras (shakes, desserts, extra fries)

- Give a Warning: *"If you break the rules, we leave!"*

- Let the children order (within the guidelines) and you order coffee or some other portable beverage (remember, you have eaten)

- Praise the children when they follow the rules

- When a child breaks the rule, calmly stand up and announce: *"You broke the rule. We are leaving."*

- Grab your coffee and walk straight to the door. Tell yourself your children are about to learn a valuable lesson. If they protest about the food, say, *"Sorry, no food is allowed in the car. There is fruit and cheese and cereal at home."* (If you like they can grab a portable, non-messy part of the meal.)

- If your kids apologize, say something obnoxious like, *"I appreciate your apology. I'll look forward to your trying harder next time."* Avoid the temptation to lecture or stop; keep walking, eyes straight ahead.

- If the children blame each other, don't feel guilty. Remember that you usually take the brunt of the blame.

- Savor this thought: parents usually never have to repeat the Trial Run once they have successfully used it.

SAYING NO and STICKING TO IT:

1 When your child first expresses his negativity—let's say he refuses to take his seat at the restaurant and announces, "There's nothing here I like,"—just ignore his remark. In a calm manner, turn to your menu and begin to discuss the food possibilities with the adults or, even better, ask one of the children who's on best behavior, *"What looks good to you?"* By ignoring your standing child, while giving attention to a cooperative child, you best help him join the group again. It may take a few minutes of ignoring for him to take his seat. As a way of saving face, he will probably dawdle and sit down very slowly. Just keep ignoring and wait him out.

2 As soon as he is seated, turn your attention to him, (don't look triumphant or overly pleased). This is probably not the moment to ask a question that could be answered with a yes or no. For example, asking "Freddy, how about your favorite—macaroni and cheese?" might invite a nasty "no" because he is angry at you and won't want to agree with you. Rather your comment should be an Invitation Back to the Family, a simple statement to him in a warm voice that lets him know the incident is over as far as you are concerned. An example might be, *"Freddy, there's one or two meals you might like here. I see macaroni and lasagna."*

3 He may take his seat, but sit like a lump, refusing to choose a meal. If so, ignore his sulking. When the server looks at your child, you may prompt him with, *"Tell the waiter what you'd like."*

If he says nothing, say calmly and firmly, *"Sounds like you want me to order for you."* Turn to the server and order something you know your child likes. If he interrupts you to order for himself, even in a grumpy tone, that's fine. Say, *"Good choice,"* and turn your attention back toward someone else or to the menu. If he is rude to the server, intervene by apologizing and then order for your child.

4 If your child does not take his seat soon, or if he appears to be flirting with breaking any of the rules, choose a Consequence. It's best to use an immediate Consequence, such as a Time-Out in the rest room or car.

Let's assess the potential effectiveness of this Consequence:

- Does a Time-Out have meaning for your child?
  Yes, most kids from two or three on up to twelve see Time-Out as a punishment.

- Do you have control over the Consequence?
  Yes, if you get up from the table, look him in the eye, say *"Come with me for a Time-Out,"* and he'll come. If he won't do it, you don't have control, so you cannot use Time-Out in public.

- Are you willing to give him a Time-Out?
  Sure. It's short, painless, and usually stops the behavior.

- Is it minimal, meaning the shortest, least punitive choice?
  Yes, one minute per year of child's age or less will be fine. Five minutes for a first offense will work for older kids.

5 Once you have chosen the Consequence, give a Warning. In this case, you might avoid a stand-off (give your child a moment or two to take his seat and save a little face) by saying, *"I am going to the rest room. Be in your seat when I come back or I will put you in Time-Out."*

6 If he is not in his seat when you return, follow through with the Time-Out.

The steps for an effective Time-Out in public are:

- Select a place for Time-Out (the rest room, the car, a corner outside or inside the restaurant).

- Go to your child, look him in the eye, and say firmly, *"Come with me for Time-Out."* Turn and head toward the bathroom or go outside the restaurant. Go slowly enough so that he can see you and follow you. You may reach for his hand, but in general it is better not to get physical in any way.

- Use your watch second hand or—if you have had problems in the past and are expecting more—carry a kitchen timer or hourglass egg timer with you.

- Ignore all your child's diversionary tactics (designed to throw you off track) like arguments, complaints, mumblings, comments like, "It's not fair!" or questions like, "Why do I have to?" Turn your body slightly away from your child, focus on something or someone else.

- When the Time-Out is over, do not lecture. Simply say, *"Your Time-Out is over. Let's go back to the table."* Calmly return to your seat.

- After your child takes his seat, wait a moment or two and then give him an Invitation Back to the Family, to show him that you are not angry and are not holding a grudge. Make sure his meal has arrived, offer him the bread, make a pleasant comment to others about something he has done recently.

- Perfect your at-home Time-Out; it's one of the secrets to an effective in-public Time-Out.

7 If Time-Out has not worked to break a pattern of obnoxious restaurant behavior, use the Consequence of taking your child and leaving the restaurant. You need to plan this carefully with your partner.

Consider the potential effectiveness of this Consequence:

- Does leaving the restaurant have meaning for your child? Most kids would rather not leave, however your child might want to, and in that case leaving would be a reward rather than an effective Consequence. If your child would want to stay at the restaurant, hire a standby baby-sitter and pick a restaurant near your home, so in the event of rotten behavior you can drop off your child at home quickly and return to enjoy your meal.

- Do you have control over leaving the restaurant?
  Most kids will not stay at a table after the parent has stood up and is moving toward the exit. You may have to carry the child, however. If you do, remain calm and make no eye contact.

- Are you willing to leave the restaurant?
  This is tricky. Even if your child is ruining the evening, you might be very ambivalent about leaving. For a Warning to be effective the child must believe you will follow through. If you would not be willing to leave, you can't threaten it.

  But if a pattern of negative behavior has occurred, you may see no other recourse than to interrupt the outing temporarily and deposit your child at home with a sitter. The good news about this Consequence is that it usually makes a great impression on your child. You won't have to do it more than once and it is very effective in changing in-public behavior.

- Is it a minimal Consequence?
  It is not overly punitive to your child, unless it is his birthday or some other very special occasion. It might be punitive to you though!

8 If you choose to use this Consequence, the Warning would be:
If you break the rules, I will take you home and you can eat with the sitter. I will come back to the restaurant.

If he breaks the rules, announce you are taking him home. You may have to carry him kicking and screaming to the car; do so as calmly as you can. Deposit him with the sitter and return to the restaurant. Make sure the sitter is one who knows how to ignore tantrums, because she can expect a whopper, at least until you have driven out of sight. And make sure she will give him attention when, and only when, he is through with his tantrum. She can give him a snack or light supper and play a game with him, for example. There should be no major fun or special privileges, no coddling or sympathizing.

9 Another version of this is for one parent to be willing to leave the party for good and take the child home. At home the parent should simply give a quick supper and put the child to bed (if it's the evening). Avoid good times and long discussions. There should be no positive payoff for his having ruined your meal. Remember, your attention is really a reward.

10 Sometimes a child will earn a Consequence and then quickly promise, "I'll be good" to avoid your following through with giving it. You certainly may accept his promise with a firm and pleasant-sounding, *"All right, I will accept your promise. Thank you."* If he then cooperates, praise him and you will probably have a good remainder of the meal. If he does not, follow-through with the original Consequence and never fall for promises again!

11 A thought about "no dessert" (as a Consequence) or "if you behave you will get dessert" (as the inspiration in a When/Then deal): While I would, in general, try to avoid using food as a punishment or reward, if you have few Consequences which have meaning for your child, you may be desperate. Try phrasing it this way: *"If you cooperate with us at the restaurant during the meal, we will stay long enough for dessert,"* or *"If you continue to scream, we will have to leave before dessert."* This will make your point, without appearing to be promising sweets.

5
Monstrous Manners in Company

THE PROBLEM:

Your child is a pain in the neck at relatives' or friends' houses (or when they are visiting you). He insists on a particular chair when it's already occupied, wants to grab food off your plate, interrupts you continuously with rude questions when you are trying to talk to your elderly aunt, kicks or bites children or adults, has a full blown flailing tantrum in the middle of the living room, announces "I'm bored" every twenty minutes, grabs toys away from—or in another way tortures—his defenseless younger cousin.

You want simply to be the parent of a model child for one day or evening. Is it so much to ask?

THINKING IT OVER:

In public, whether stranger-public, friend-public, or family-public, kids often display their most creative and challenging obnoxious behaviors. In fact, in these circumstances you frequently see behavior your child would never, and I mean never, pull otherwise. It's as if our kids know we are on trial for Felony Poor Parenting and we've got the most unsympathetic jury in the world.

With family, the pressure is on in full. We're excited to see everyone. We fantasize happily catching up and the kids getting along perfectly, all one big happy family. WRONG!

Yes, you do have a right to a peaceful gathering, and yes, such gatherings are stressful for kids of all ages. When kids are stressed they call upon us more. And they act up more. But no one member, no matter how small, should wreck the day for the rest of the family. And if you do nothing, your family and friends will justifiably be annoyed.

So what to do? Remember the virtues of preparation and limit-setting. Establish a visiting routine with clear expectations for your kids to follow, then use your limit-setting tools in the trenches. No one will fault you for taking charge of a bad situation. In fact, your family will be a little in awe of you perhaps, grateful to you certainly, and may even ask you for advice with their kids.

GETTING PERFECT BEHAVIOR (Will you settle for Reasonable Behavior?):

1 In your own home let your child know what rude behavior is and what the Consequence will be for rude behavior. If at dinner he says, "Yuck, this tastes awful," respond with, *"You are insulting my cooking and that's being rude. The next time you are rude, you will leave the table for three minutes."*

2 Insist on good behavior when visiting anyone at any time, whether it's a short coffee visit with a neighbor or dropping something off at a friend's. Small trips serve as practice for longer ones. Establish clear rules and if they are violated give a Warning of a Consequence, such as the removal of a privilege (no TV, no dessert, or early bedtime). If your child starts to cooperate, thank him. If not, follow-through with the Consequence. To further drive home the point, you may leave the child with a sitter or his other parent the next time you run errands. If your child begs to go, you might say:

The last time we went to the bakery, you kept interrupting me when I was ordering. Today you must stay home. I'll give you another chance next Saturday.

He may scream until you are out of sight, but my guess is he will try harder on errands in the future. And that better behavior will carry over to other outings.

3 If visiting others' homes tends to be difficult for your child, or if you want to cut trouble off at the pass, assess the upcoming event. Consider these and other possible problems and interventions:

- If the party is starting during your child's nap time, arrive late, after nap, or early enough so he can nap on the way or before all the family arrives.

- If the party is starting later than his meal time, have snacks in the car or bring along a sack lunch for him to have whenever he needs it.

- If the gathering is around a dinner table, light candles. A dimly lit room often has a soothing effect on kids. And since they love to blow out candles, use this When/Then Deal: *"Whoever remembers their manners at dinner tonight gets to blow out the candles."* (If there are more terrific diners than candles, re-light for round two.) Be specific about what "good manners" mean to you, i.e., no reaching, chewing with mouth closed, and staying seated during the meal.

- If Cousin Albert hates to share his toys, bring along some of your child's toys. Choose toys he's willing to share with Albert, toys that could get lost or wrecked without major trauma.

- If your child is at an age when he hates to share his mom or dad and you are looking forward to spending time talking with Aunt Margaret, hire an older cousin to play with him for an hour or two, and rent a video he is fond of for after dinner.

- If the party will last past his bedtime, bring a sleeping bag, pj's, toothbrush, and teddy bear. He can either bed down at his usual time or when he gets tired and cranky. Or you can choose to leave early and bundle him into the car all ready to plop into bed.

- If your plan is to put your child to bed while the party is still going on, both Dad and Mom should spend some separate relaxed, relatively brief, "good-night time," so that he gets as much of his normal routine with stories, lullabies, and so forth, as possible.

- If your child is not fond of the cousins, or vice versa, "inspire cooperation" with a When/Then Deal: *"Hey, if you can get along with your cousins tonight, you can have a friend sleep over tomorrow night."* In case the kids need to play separately, bring along books or other solitary play things, such as cards for solitaire, music tapes, or art supplies.

- If you are planning to visit a friend or relative your child has never met, prepare him as best you can by letting him know what to expect. A few short talks can include this type of information:

  Cousin Lloyd lives in a house with an upstairs and a downstairs. There will be lots of people there, cooking and eating and talking. Your aunts will probably want to kiss you and you don't have to like it.

  Uncle Malcolm likes to wrestle. You will probably like that a lot, but if he tickles you too much, tell him you don't like it or call me. He used to tickle me a lot when we were kids.

  You may be bored until the big cousins arrive. Take a couple of books and your headset, why don't you?

4 Establish the rules before you go. Pick the three most important ones and make them clear to your child:

Keep your feet off the furniture.

If your aunt gives you food you don't like, don't announce you don't like it, just leave it on your plate.

Please say "Excuse me," if you need to interrupt.

If he follows the rules, praise him with a whisper in his ear, a thumb's up sign, or a big hug for any terrific visiting behavior.

5 Let your child know what family subjects are taboo or "private," that is, might be embarrassing or hurtful for someone if they were brought up, such as a teen cousin's pregnancy, Uncle Bud's hair loss from chemotherapy, or bickering that goes on between a couple near divorce. Let him know that if he is curious or concerned or frightened you will gladly talk with him privately about his worries.

6 Give your relatives permission to set limits, if they have similar parenting styles. It is sometimes easiest to defer to them. Even better than your saying, "Aunt Nancy does not allow jumping on the furniture. If you do that again, you will have to play outside," get Aunt Nancy to say, *"If you jump on the furniture in my house, you will need to play outside for fifteen minutes."* Nancy will probably be pleased that you respect her rules and you will be off the hook a bit.

7 Before a big event, say a wedding, about which you are nervous, plan a Trial Run or two in preparation. Any low-stress event, such as a close friend's pot luck, relaxed Sunday walk with neighbors, or an afternoon barbecue in the park, can provide a perfect opportunity to practice reasonable behavior. Do the Trial Run following these guidelines:

• Remind your child of the rules (three is a good number):

> *Keep your hands to yourself with Tony.*
> *No pulling the cat's tail or chasing the dog.*
> *Do not leave the Sims' yard without asking Dad or Mom.*

- Give a Warning of a Consequence (See Glossary for definition of effective Consequence), for example:
  Remember, if you break the rules, you will go to bed half an hour early.

- Praise your child for following any of the rules:
  Hey, guys, you are playing together so well. Thanks!

  You're being so nice and gentle with Woofer.

  Good job remembering to ask before going to the park.

- If he breaks a rule, follow through with the Consequence:
  You left the yard without asking. Tonight, bedtime is at 7:30 sharp.

- Have another Trial Run before the big event, such as a pot luck at your house, and again, announce the Consequence for breaking any of the rules. Pick a Consequence you will be able to enforce while hosting the party. Give the Consequence if your child earns it. The Trial Run will give you confidence in public and give your child the valuable message, "My parent means business."

8 If you have prepared for the outing as I have suggested, you may find that your child really rises to the occasion and behaves well, because you have prepared yourself for the worst.

In my private practice, clients often bring up situations which daunt them, such as when family reunions are approaching. We go over what is troubling them and strategize ways to handle difficult people or situations. Next we practice together for the upcoming event, for example, a woman will plan to ignore—by changing the subject—her father's unkind comments about her spouse. If her father continues, she plans to leave the room calmly. Often, after the visit, the client returns saying something like, "Dad wasn't all that bad this time."

I am convinced that part of the reason "Dad wasn't all that bad" is that he picked up an unspoken but perceptible change in his daughter. She was prepared this time to handle him if he became rude or insulting. She was not going to tolerate it.

In the same way, your preparations can give your child the message that rude or aggressive behaviors will not be tolerated. Your messages, spoken or not, are communicated to your child and can effect his behavior.

If, in spite of all preparation, a rule is broken, follow through with your limit-setting plans.

SAYING NO and STICKING TO IT:

1 As this outing is a treat for you—or you were hoping it would be—do not cut your day or evening short in response to your child's tantrum. He may have to suffer the Consequence of an early bedtime, docking of his allowance, losing out on a favorite TV show, or missing dessert (if that is the only Consequence you have at hand). Don't ever reward outrageous behavior by punishing yourself!

2 If you need an immediate, all-purpose, portable Consequence, try using Time-Out. (See Glossary.) Time-Out meets all the criteria of an effective Consequence:

- It has meaning for the child (kids usually hate it).

- Parents usually can get their child to take Time-Out (so they have the necessary control).

- Parents are willing to give Time-Out (it's not overly punitive).

- Time-Out is minimal (it is brief and immediate).

3 Remind your child of the rules and give him a Warning that he will earn Time-Out if he breaks a rule.

4 Praise your child if he cooperates with following the rules, but if he breaks a rule, lead him (or calmly carry him if necessary) out of the family area and give him Time-Out. If you need to stay with him so that he won't be scared, do so, but turn away and do not interact with him. You needn't demand silence, just that he is in the chair for a specified short time.

5 If he refuses to stay in the chair, use a room with no fun or danger potential. Lead him to the room, leave the door ajar, and wait just outside the door for the appropriate number of minutes (two minutes would be fine for a two to six-year-old). Use your watch or, if possible, a kitchen timer. When the timer rings simply give him an Invitation Back to the Family, *"Your Time-Out is over. You may come join the family now."*

6 Don't lecture or remind him of his transgressions. Wipe the slate clean and start afresh. If he sits sulking and refuses to budge, let him know where you will be in a pleasant, non-punitive tone, *"I'll be sitting with Nana on the front porch."*

7 Every time he repeats the offense that day or in the subsequent days on a longer trip, he earns another Time-Out. You may increase the time slightly.

8 Remember that, even more than in your day-to-day life at home, on trips of any length your child needs clear expectations and firm, fair limit-setting.

For Their Own Good

Picture our kids living the life they'd
choose. One long junk food video
vacation and civilization crumbling
around us. Face it, folks, we can't leave
them to their own devices.

6
Balking at Bedtime

THE PROBLEM:

Your child refuses to go to bed and stay in bed. He gets up or calls you to his bedside, asks for water, says he's hungry, insists he's not tired, argues that his friends don't have to go to bed as early, wants to read or play, says he's sick (which he is not), begs to sleep with you, or just cries and screams to be allowed out of bed. You want peace and quiet in the evening and a good night's sleep. You want your child to go to bed, stay in bed, maybe even fall asleep at a reasonable hour.

THINKING IT OVER:

Children need a good night's sleep (and so do parents!) and they seem to do best with a regular and predictable bedtime routine and a night's sleep in their own beds. Most parents report to me that their children do not "sleep in" after staying up late, so they don't "make up" for a late night the way we adults do. They awake at about the same time, irritable and cranky. Their internal clocks may not be alarm clocks but sundials, as they seem to wake to the amount of light in the room, rather than when their bodies are rested.

In order for your child to get a clear message about bedtime, both parents need to agree on and send the same, clear message,

"We want you to go to bed and stay in bed." You and your partner, however, may not agree. Maybe you would like a regular bedtime, while your partner thinks a child falls asleep when he needs to. Or perhaps you want an early bedtime, while your partner would like more time to play with the little guy after dinner. You may not mind your toddler joining you in bed in the middle of the night, but your partner might have something else in mind. The first step in solving the bedtime problem, then, is for the two of you to talk about it and arrive at a bedtime plan you can both live with and carry out consistently.

To help you, check with your pediatrician as to the amount of sleep she recommends for your child. Take your child's own patterns into account; he may need less sleep or more sleep than children his age and size. Your child's teacher's observations may help you, too. How is he doing at school? Is he alert or sleepy in the morning?

Once you have ascertained how much sleep your child ideally should get, set a regular bedtime. Do the best you can, considering the time you get home from work. Streamline dinner preparation or bath time. Cut out weekday TV time altogether (except if it helps you get dinner on the table or a younger sibling to bed). Have your child do his homework as soon as he gets home or at his after-school care (you can review the work after dinner). Your goal is to allow your child the bedtime his body needs, the family time you all need, and the personal time you and your partner need.

HOW TO GET YOUR CHILD TO GO TO BED:

1 Make a plan for the evening. Work backwards from the time you want "lights out for good." Write down what you need to accomplish and when those tasks need to be started or completed. Be realistic about time allotments. If you think you can do it in five minutes, allow eight.

A toddler might have the following bedtime routine:
    Bath at 6:30
    Pajamas and teeth brushing at 6:50
    Story or lullabies at 7:00
    Goodnight's to family and bedroom "friends" at 7:15
    Final sip of water at 7:18
    Mom and Dad out of the room at 7:20

  A school-age child could have this routine:
    Dinner and homework done by 7:15
    Washed up, teeth brushed, and pajamas on by 7:30
    Reading, games, or TV until 7:58
    In bed by 8:00
    Reading to self or with parent, then goodnights by 8:29
    Lights out by 8:30

Take into consideration everything you and your child need to do to be ready for school or child care in the morning: packing backpack, making school lunch, selecting and laying out clothes, putting toys away, and so forth.

You can post four or five of the tasks in words or pictures on the refrigerator or his bedroom door to help him get a sense of the nightly plan, but don't expect your child to organize his time himself. After all, your schedule might be good for him, but it is your schedule. He won't be motivated to remember it and he will need reminders.

2 Once you have planned your schedule, stick to it. When your child is small it's easier to be consistent. By the time they are school-age, children have more homework, resist going to bed when it's still light outside, have television programs that they want to watch, and will debate "but my friends stay up 'til 9:30!" Put a plan into place when your child is young, and adjust it appropriately as he gets older.

3 Put a short, quiet, family time, such as reading, watching TV or playing a favorite game, in between the pj's, brushing and flossing, etc., and going to bed. It's a lot more inspiring for your kids to hear, *"OK, guys, pajamas and teeth and climb up on my bed for stories!"* than "OK, guys, pajamas and teeth and into bed!"

Or if you can't spare the extra time, use a When/Then Deal, with the offer of a fun, solitary activity to help him stick to the schedule: *"When you are all ready for bed—and that means pajamas on, teeth brushed and your backpack packed—you can draw, play solitaire, or sort your comic cards for twenty minutes."*

4 Give an Announcement a few minutes before transition times—times when you need to interrupt your child's play or reading. An Announcement might be, *"In five minutes it will be time to put your toys away and brush your teeth,"* or *"You have five more minutes reading time before 'lights out.'"*

5 Don't insist on leaving the lights on or off, the door open or shut, or even the covers pulled up in the cold or down in the heat. This is a time for choosing your battles. You don't need to win every skirmish and your child may need a small face-saving victory by the end of the day. After he is asleep you can cover him up, turn on the nightlight, or open the door.

6 Don't stay in your child's room waiting for him to fall asleep. It is easy to start the habit of laying down with your child or sitting by his bed. It's comforting for him and relaxing for you. Many children's sleep problems, however, grow out of their inability to fall asleep by themselves. Even a baby needs to learn to fall asleep unaided.

7 Avoid creating a bedtime ritual which includes too many steps. One family had an hour "goodnight" which included a drink of water, many minutes of backscratching, a book or two, a "story without pages" (lovely name for a made-up story), and Mom sitting in the room until the child was asleep. Once Mom and Dad agreed they both needed a change, they were successful in weaning their child from the hour "goodnight" to a twenty minute one.

Likewise, avoid long stretches of backscratching or rubbing. Sure, two or five or ten minutes is fine, but if every night your child demands you sit at his bed for a half-hour or more until he falls asleep, that's going too far.

8 Avoid having your child sleep the night in your bed with you. It starts innocently enough—dear little bundle of nursing baby, ridiculously tired mom. Who could exile a baby to his own room? But days turn into months very quickly. Soon years are passing and your little guy is somewhere on the continuum from always in parents' bed to frequently in parents' bed.

As your child gets older, it becomes harder to break bedtime habits. I recommend that, as much as possible, your baby should sleep in his own bed. If he falls asleep nursing with you, put him back in his crib after you burp him. Both of you need to be in the habit of returning baby to his bed, even if he starts out with you.

If, like some families, you enjoy the "family bed" concept, having babies and toddlers join you for the night, keep in mind that at some point you will need to regain your privacy and your child will need to learn to be independent from you at night.

9 Don't wrestle or tickle or do other very stimulating activity right before bedtime. Your kid will be bouncing off the walls and bedtime will be a lot tougher. Wrestle earlier in the evening or, better yet, in the morning!

10 Everyone likes to be tucked in bed and kissed goodnight. So for final lights out, be at your child's bedside. If he keeps getting up, forget about the bedside bit. You only get one tuck-in a night!

11 Praise your child for complying at any stage of the bedtime routine. Examples are:

Wow! You got undressed so fast tonight!

Thanks for putting your clothes in the hamper.

You stayed in bed after 'night-nights' last night. That was terrific!

SAYING NO and STICKING TO IT:

1 If your child has less than stellar bedtimes habits (or if you need to get back on track after a period of illness or other stressful event), sit down with him in a little Family Meeting and tell him there is going to be a change. For example, if his birthday is coming up you can say, *"Next month you are going to be four years old. When you are four you will be ready go to sleep without Mommy or Daddy sitting beside your bed until you fall asleep."*

After he has turned four (or whatever), remind him of the conversation you had and implement the change. Announce, *"I'll stay with you for a little while, then I have to go make a phone call (do the dishes, visit with Daddy...). Later on I'll come back to check on you. Soon you will learn to fall asleep by yourself."*

Use a weaning procedure to shorten the amount of time you sit with him. Steps might be:

- Stay until he is almost asleep. Give him a quiet kiss and say, *"I need to talk to Dad now, I'll be back to check on you in a few minutes. Goodnight, sweetheart."*

- Return to the room periodically until he is asleep. Give a quiet word or two or just a pat on the back. If he argues, cries, or complains, say, *"If you can lie quietly I'll come back to check on you, but if you fuss, I won't."*

- Shorten the amount of time you spend sitting at his bed by five minute increments until he can tolerate five minutes.

Promise you will be back to check on him in a little while and say gently, but firmly, *"Good night."*

2 In every bedtime situation give a clear Command: *You must stay in bed now and be quiet. Goodnight, sweetheart.*

3 If he gets out of bed, give a Reminder: *Go back to bed and stay in bed.*

4 If he calls, cries or screams, tell him you're going to ignore his calls:

It's time to go to sleep. You've had your water, your story, your kiss and your hug. If you call me again, I will not answer you.

If he stays quietly in bed for ten minutes, you may tiptoe in and give an extra kiss. Say, *"You're doing a great job staying in bed. See you in the morning."* If you find that returning to praise him stirs him up, don't do it!

5 If he keeps getting out of bed, you have three tools to help you ignore:

- Calmly walk or carry your child back to his bed. I emphasize the word calmly. Your anger or frustration will not induce sleep. Don't talk to him, cuddle him or interact. Don't make eye contact until you place him in bed and quietly but firmly command, *"Stay in bed."* Go back to what you were doing. Repeat this until he gives up. (Keep saying to yourself, *"I can ignore. I can ignore. I can ignore."*)

- Try the Broken Record Technique. When he comes into the room, make eye contact and say, *"Back to bed."* Respond to every argument with the exact same phrase, *"Back to bed."* Say nothing except *"Back to bed"* until he gets frustrated and stomps off. Repeat if he comes out again. Ignore the crying or yelling that may ensue for a couple of nights until he gets the message.

• Ignore his presence completely. Let's say he's crept into the living room. Don't look at him. Don't answer questions, don't yell, don't lecture. Focus on something else, such as the newspaper or your conversation with your partner. If you and all adults in the room do this, he will most likely leave the unwelcome atmosphere and creep back to bed or fall asleep on the floor by your feet. The ignoring will not work, however, if you have the television on. He may just join in the watching.

6 If he gives a full blown tantrum, ignore as if your life depended upon it. I promise you, you won't have to do this many nights. Plan ahead for an evening of digging in your heels and ignoring until he falls asleep. Start the bedtime retraining on a Friday night. Have a terrific juicy novel, a magazine full of gossip or a challenging crossword puzzle, anything which can hold your attention. Get lots of sleep the night before. Use earplugs if you need them. Stay focused on your book or project or pretend to. Repeat to yourself, *"I can outlast him. It will take just one or two nights. I can do it."*

Repeat the same bedtime procedure each night until your child gets the picture.

7 If he turns on the light and continues to play or read, enter his room and calmly but firmly repeat the Command, *"It's time to turn off your light."* Allow him a moment or two to turn it off himself. If he does not, say, *"Will you turn off the light or shall I?"* He may grumpily do so, but if not, turn it off yourself. Ignore the screams that follow.

8 If he tries to bargain for a later bedtime, tell him, *"It's too late to decide that tonight. I will be happy to discuss it tomorrow. Goodnight."* Respond to any other comment with, *"The subject is closed, goodnight."*

The next day, when he brings up the subject of a later bedtime, you can certainly discuss the matter. Perhaps you or he can call the pediatrician to see what bedtime she recommends. If the issue is that your child is grumpy in the morning, you might offer a When/Then Deal: *"Let's try an 8:30 bedtime tonight. If you wake up easily and get ready for school on time, then I'll know you can handle an 8:30 bedtime. If not, we'll both know you really still need that extra half-hour of rest."*

9 If he keeps arguing or resisting, give a Warning of a Consequence such as, *"For every minute you stay up past your bedtime tonight, you will go to bed that many minutes earlier tomorrow night."* Be sure to follow though the next night.

10 You may consider allowing him to stay up later reading or playing quietly in his room for fifteen or twenty minutes, if your main concern is gaining some adult personal time. You might indeed be happy with your child just resting. Let him know that you are "off duty" as a parent (except of course, for emergencies).

11 If your child wakes with a nightmare and calls you, go to him rather than have him come to you. Stay with him a bit to soothe and calm him, but return alone to your bed. Try not to get in the habit of falling asleep in his bed; again, this will just increase his dependence upon you.

When my children would come into my room with nightmares and ask to sleep with me, I would say, *"You can visit for a few minutes, but then I am going to take you back to your room."* With that preparation, they were able to accept the move back to their own beds five minutes later. The danger in this, however, is that you might fall asleep in those couple of minutes. Use this technique with extreme caution!

12 Praise your child when he goes to bed on time. In the morning congratulate him or rave about it to the family depending upon his age. Give him a star on a Better Behavior Chart and perhaps even a small reward or privilege. Warning: Don't have the reward be staying up later the next night!

13 There are excellent sleep books on the market for children and babies who have a particularly hard time going to sleep.

7
Homework Resistance

THE PROBLEM:

Your child resists doing his homework. He forgets his assignments or says he has none, leaves his books at school, puts off doing the homework or does it in a slipshod manner, neglects to get the finished work into his backpack, or fails to turn it in to the teacher.

You want your child to take responsibility for his work. Is that really so much to ask?

THINKING IT OVER:

You want to do your job as a parent, but are sick of nagging your child about his homework. Even if you are willing to coax him through daily assignments, every so often he wakes up in a panic screaming, "My life is over. I forgot! I'm having a social studies test today."

"Should I bail him out?" you wonder. The capital of Uruguay floats to consciousness, but what are the major exports—corn or coffee beans, bauxite or bananas? You hear a groan, "And I didn't bring my book home!" Even if you wanted to help, you can't.

To make matters worse, each teacher seems to give a different message about homework. His first grade teacher didn't believe in it and his second loaded it on. The third grade teacher gives homework, but if a child doesn't finish, she says sweetly, "That's okay, you'll have time in class." You hear rumors that next year's teacher is quite harsh on kids who do not complete assignments.

For your child to feel that schoolwork is important he needs a clear message from both parents. But perhaps you and your partner do not see eye-to-eye on homework. She or he was not a stellar student and says, "I turned out okay. Give him time." Or "Schoolwork should be done at school—after school is playtime." It's not that your partner doesn't have a good point, but that the two of you need to come to an accord. If either of you were lucky enough to succeed in spite of school problems, you are the exception and not the rule (and those were the good old days).

One of the advantages of a child's doing homework is that it gives him an opportunity to develop responsibility in a setting outside the home. Remembering assignments, organizing materials, gathering information, and budgeting time are just some of the many important skills he will need his whole life. Take heart! It's not all on your shoulders; the teacher shares the weight.

Certainly your child needs a good education. And in order to get a good education, sooner or later he is going to have to face the music and be responsible for his in-class and at-home work. Let's look at some ways you can help him develop responsible school habits.

HOW TO GET STRUGGLE FREE HOMEWORK:

1 From early on in your child's school life, set an example for him by taking his schoolwork seriously. You can indicate how important school is in several ways:

- Ask your child about his day. You may have to get creative here. The standard questions, "How was school?" or "What happened in school today?" are met with the respective responses "Fine" and "Nothing." To get the memory juices to start flowing a bit, ask: *"Anything strange (funny, scary, awful, silly, new, disappointing, embarrassing, boring) happen at school today?"*

- Visit the classroom whenever you can. Most teachers welcome your presence. If you can spare twenty minutes to read, an hour to help with art, a half-day to tutor or lead a special class, your child will love it and you will learn about his day and his teacher's style.

- Get to know the teacher by phone, if you cannot meet with her in person. Teachers often are willing to accommodate parents' schedules. Yes, it may be inconvenient for them, but they usually welcome your interest.

- Attend school events and activities as frequently as you can. When parents are involved—attend PTA meetings or Open Houses, volunteer or fundraise—their children benefit in the classroom. Most events are held during the daytime, but as more parents work full-time, many schools are trying to schedule more evening events.

2 You can give the message that school, and therefore schoolwork, is important by insisting that your child go to bed early (to get enough sleep for school), arrive on time, dress appropriately (by school standards), and carry the proper tools that he needs (backpack, pencils, assignment book etc.).

3 Set a regular time for homework; after school is ideal. Children work more efficiently and are still full of energy at three or four o'clock. If your child is in an after-school program where he can start his homework, that is great. If everyone arrives home at six or later, have your child start while you prepare dinner.

4 Practice the rule, like the When/Then Deal: *"First you work, then you play."* Insist that your child completes his work before going out to play, watching TV, or talking on the telephone. Once your child is outside or in front of the TV, it will be a lot harder for him to get to work. If your child has lots of homework and you'd like him to have a little play time, have him work an hour, play an hour, then finish up the homework.

Feel free to eliminate TV altogether during the week. It reduces nightly confrontations. Or purchase a VCR to record favorite TV fare. Use the taped programs on weekends after completing chores. Fast-forward during commercials; think of the time you save and the sales-pitching you have avoided!

5 Establish the importance of homework by having a regular place for your child to work. I like the kitchen or dining room table—the center of the home. Kids may feel a bit isolated off in their room. Many a family has gone to the trouble of getting a desk, lamp, and so forth arranged in the bedroom, only to find their child prefers to hang out with the family. As long as your child can work midst a little distraction, the kitchen table works terrifically. Your eleven or twelve-year-old may prefer studying in his room. That's fine, just watch out for TV or other electronic interference.

6 Provide your child the tools he will need. Have a drawer or box near the homework place for pencils, pens, markers, an eraser, stapler, glue, paper, scotch tape, a dictionary, a ruler, a pencil sharpener, etc. Insist that he put his materials away in the drawer so they are always ready to use for homework.

7 Find out your child's teacher's expectations about homework in the first few days of school. If you are unable to see her in person, call on the phone or send a letter via your child with a request for a response. Leave your phone number and times you can be reached. Tell the teacher you need to know:

- How much time she expects your child to spend on homework each evening.

- How much help or guidance she expects parents to give. Does she expect that the parent will review and have the child correct his mistakes or not?

- If your child is taking longer to do the homework than the teacher recommends, what would the teacher have him do? Work until it's done, no matter how long it takes, or bring in unfinished work? (If this is a recurring problem, you need to assess the teacher's accuracy in gauging the time required to do the assignment or if your child has learning problems. Another gauge is how much time other classmates are spending on the same assignment.)

- What are the repercussions for not completing homework assignments?

8 Show interest in your child's work and projects. Ask about the assignments, review returned work, schedule trips to do research in the library. Note long term assignments on a family calendar or post them on the refrigerator. Give Reminders (friendly, non nagging ones).

9 To inspire neatness, praise the neater parts of papers, while ignoring the messier parts. We tend to harp on the erasure marks, the penmanship, the tear in the paper. Listen to the difference in the following examples of parent feedback to a somewhat messy paper. This would be terrible feedback: "You've done a very sloppy job on this paper, Ricky." It would be so inspiring to say: *"This first line here, Ricky, this is great. Your letters all stayed right on the line."* In the second example Dad praised the "small step in the right direction," taking advantage of his child's line or two of neat writing to encourage more. Which response is more likely to help improve Ricky's work?

10 Likewise, focus on what's correct, rather than what is not. Think of the difference in these two comments from the child's perspective: "You got three wrong. What a shame. Almost a perfect paper." or *"Ninety-seven right! Do you ever know your multiplication or what!"*

11 To get your child to work more independently, give him small tasks and have him call you when he's finished. In this way you decrease his dependence on you.

> *Do the first row of your math problems. When you're done, call me....[William does so]...Wow, you sure finished those quickly, William. Let's go over them and then you can try two more rows.*

With a child who has demanded you sit with him while he does all his homework, say, *"Do one problem and then call me."* He finishes the one, calls you, and you check the answer. Say something like, *"Great job. Now do two problems and call me."* When your child is able to work on his own, say *"Fantastic, you finished all those math problems by yourself."*

12 Ask your child about his teacher's response to his homework.

> *What did she think of your poem?...How did she like the model of the Inuit igloo?...What did she say about your interview of our letter carrier?*

If your teacher does not give feedback, that is a serious problem which will interfere with your child's ability to take pride in his work. Consult the teacher immediately. If she does not begin to give some response to the child for his work, speak to the principal and consider a move to another classroom.

13 Make sure your child has other responsibilities in the home. A teacher friend said that her number one secret to cutting homework resistance is to make sure he has at least one daily household chore to do. Chores help children develop a sense of responsibility and this helps a child in doing homework.

SAYING NO and STICKING TO IT:

1 If your child begins to struggle at homework, work below his potential, or fail at school, first rule out the possibility of learning disabilities or attention problems. Kids can be smart but also have "processing problems," that is they have trouble taking in or putting out information. This can mean difficulty in understanding, synthesizing, or communicating. It can effect reading, writing, math, oral skills, and more. If you have any concern at all that your child may be suffering from an undiagnosed learning disability, talk to your teacher and request that the school district's educational psychologist test your child.

Likewise, if your child has trouble staying on task, following directions, or completing work, he may have Attention Deficit Hyperactivity Disorder which interferes significantly with a child's ability to pay attention and learn. A child psychiatrist is best qualified to diagnose or rule out this disorder.

2 If your child's homework failure is sudden and if you also see a decreased interest in playing with friends and sleeping or eating problems, your child may be suffering from depression. Consult your child's physician or a child psychiatrist immediately.

3 If problems are in homework only, answer the following:

- Is your child writing down the assignment?
  If not, he needs an assignment notebook.

- Is your child writing it down correctly?
  If not, have the teacher read it and initial it.

- Is he bringing the assignment book home?
  If not, he needs to tie the notebook to his backpack.

- Is he bringing home all necessary books or materials?
  If not, perhaps the teacher can give him prompts or he can

have a more detailed assignment sheet with a column for remembering materials and books to bring home.

- Is he doing the work?
  If not, find out what he is doing instead—then see below.

- Is the finished work getting into the backpack?
  If not, he should put it into his backpack when it's done.

- Is the work getting to the teacher?
  If not, perhaps your teacher needs to ask for it or provide a column on his assignment sheet for the teacher to initial having received the work.

Teachers do not have a lot of time to write notes home and follow up, but if your child is having trouble, she should be willing to quickly scrawl her initials once or twice in order to help him. The skills I have listed are your school's responsibility to teach in the elementary grades. If your teacher is not willing to assist in this way, the principal needs to know.

4 Rather than struggle with your eight to twelve-year-old child about homework, try the "What's Your Plan" approach:
Carl, you need to do a few chores and I know you've got a book report to complete. Tonight your favorite show is on. I was wondering what your plan is for getting it done?

If he comes up with, "I'll get up tomorrow morning early," say, *"That might work, but you really need to get it done tonight."*
I tried the "What's Your Plan?" with Kyle when he was eight and we had this dialogue:

Mom: I know you want to go out to play but you've got homework to do. What's your plan for doing it?

Kyle: How about I go over to David's to play and come back in forty minutes?

Mom: Well, that's not a lot of time to play.

Kyle: Yes, it is.

Mom: If it seems like enough time to you, okay. But how will you know what time it is?

Kyle: I'll bring a watch.

Mom: Good thinking, but what if you forget to look at your watch?

Kyle: Mom, I promise, if I come back late, then tomorrow I'll just have to get my homework done before I go out.

I was shocked and pleased when he presented his plan and the very logical Consequence. Kyle did come home when the forty minutes were up and he did do his homework without a word. I think the plan worked because he picked his own way to solve the problem.

If your child does not come up with a workable plan, or if he does not follow through with it, then abandon the "What's Your Plan" approach. Try again in another six months or so.

5 Set up a Better Behavior Chart (see Glossary) to count and celebrate homework completion. Give a sticker when your child puts the completed work into his backpack. Leave the space blank if he doesn't earn a sticker. Praise the successes. Ignore the failures.

Tie the stickers to a reward which he can collect on the weekend. If each day's sticker is worth ten cents, he can have up to fifty cents added to his allowance on Saturday or two quarters for video games when you go to the grocery store.

6 Find out what is getting in the way and get it out of the way! Is your child avoiding homework to play outside, watch TV, work on the computer, play video games, talk on the telephone, or read? Reestablish and stick by the When/Then Deal:

When your homework is done, then you may play.

With a chronic homework resister, do not give in to nagging and do not accept promises to "do it later," if those very same promises have been broken time and time again. You must be the Bad Guy and enforce the rule. Think, "Consistency, consistency, consistency."

If you are not at home in the afternoon, and don't have a sitter or after-school child care worker who can effectively manage your child's use of his time, the rule might be, *"As soon as I am home, you must come in from play and start homework."* Have an effective Consequence in mind if he does not do so.

7 If you are too exhausted, get home too late from work, are a single parent, or just feel helpless in the homework struggle, reach out to the teacher for support. Consider this plan which has worked for other families:

- Meet with your child's teacher, letting her know that you are very concerned with the homework problem. Tell her the steps you have tried and see what ideas she has. If you have the strength to continue to try to intervene, do so.

- If not, ask the teacher what Consequence she gives a child for not turning in homework. An appropriate Consequence, such as staying in at recess and lunch break until the homework is done, needs to meet the following criteria:

  It's meaningful to the child (your kid loves recess).

  The teacher has control over it (she can stay with the child in the classroom or take him to the office to work).

  You're willing to use it (it's not overly punitive).

  It's minimal (brief, can be used daily).

  If the Consequence your teacher usually gives does not meet these criteria, ask her to consider another Consequence. Some teachers assign writing "standards" (i.e., having child write one hundred times, "I will complete my homework on time."). This Consequence might be meaningful to your child (he hates to write standards!) and the teacher may be able to make your child write them, but in my opinion, it fails the "willingness" test. If my child was not getting his homework done, the last thing he would need is busywork which has no learning value at all. Because I would not be willing to have that Consequence used, I might undermine its effectiveness in some way. I might go so far as to help my child finish his homework, because I thought his writing standards the next day would be a waste of time!

Other teachers might give the child the Consequence of a grade of "F" for the incomplete homework. Although it is important that the child have a Consequence, the "F" grade would fail my "minimal" test. I would like to see another consequence tried first, such as reducing the grade for every day late (an "A" paper due on Monday would be reduced to "B" if turned in on Tuesday and then "C" if turned in on Wednesday and so forth).

- If you and the teacher can agree on a Consequence, tell her you "want out" of the battle. Explain to the teacher that your begging, pleading, threatening, helping, and screaming are not working. You want your child to face the music at school and you want his teacher to adopt the role of disciplinarian. Let all the natural consequences occur: staying in at recess, disappointing playmates, garnering embarrassment from buddies, and of course eventually, the positive reinforcement of finishing the assignment. Reassure the teacher that you take your child's education very seriously and that you would not put it in her hands if you felt that you had any other choice.

It may be hard for you to remove yourself from the homework struggle. Remember that your battling or finishing the homework for him is not going to do the trick and that you may have to disengage for him to change his habits. The responsibility must shift from you to him.

- At home, ignore his homework avoidance. You know that he will have to do it at school the next day or face another Consequence. Keep the policy, *"No TV until homework is done."* Other privileges? That's up to you.

    It is far better for a child to experience the natural consequences of his not doing homework (staying in at recess to finish, getting poor grades on a report card, or having a conference with parents and teacher) in elementary or middle school, rather than later in high school or college.

- Remain interested in your child's school and schoolwork. Be prepared to praise accomplishment. Bask in the freedom as the teacher does the dirty work. This may be the last flexible teacher you get!

8 Avoid setting up long term rewards, such as, "I'll give you $50 for an all A/B report card. Or "I'll take you to ———(major amusement park of your choice) if you bring your fails up to passing." Your child will have a hard time striving toward a goal that will take ten weeks to accomplish. It is better to reward the nightly completion of homework with praise or a small privilege. School achievement is based on developing a variety of good study habits and having many small successes.

8

Too Much TV

THE PROBLEM:

Your child refuses to turn off the TV. She insists on watching at meals or before school. You are so sick of the thing you want to give it away. You want TV use not TV abuse.

THINKING IT OVER:

Many of us have a love-hate relationship with television. Reluctantly we introduce *Sesame Street* to our toddler in order to get a shower or a private moment in the bathroom. Soon we are playing a video in the den to have a child-free dinner party in the dining room. We know it is possible for TV to be a great educator or entertainer, but the exposure to violence, adult themes, offensive language, and downright stupidity concerns us. And teachers have found that children with reading problems watch many hours of TV weekly.

If we watch TV with our children, it may help them develop an understanding of what they see and a healthy distrust of commercialism, but who has time to monitor their watching?

And what about the time wasted! Remember reading, drawing, playing marbles, singing, storytelling, or cross-stitching? What about imaginary play, or just soaking up sunshine and fresh air?

The more time spent in front of the TV the less time and interest children have for other productive pastimes.

"But," you wonder, "How do I get the TV monster back in the cage? I know we'd be doing them a favor by limiting TV, but who wants to be The Enforcer?"

Repeat after me, "I have a right to limit TV. In fact, it's my responsibility." And read-on.

WARNING: If you or your partner is addicted to TV, you will have to change your habits first, before you can be effective with the kids.

HOW TO WEAN KIDS FROM TV:

1 Show a particular interest in any non-TV activity your child does. She'll learn to value what you value. Say things like:

That looks like a great book, tell me about it.

What a tall tower you're making with those blocks!

Bugs? Sure you can collect bugs. Let me show you the good places to dig.

I love the colors in your drawing. When it's done, can we hang it on the refrigerator?

2 Pinpoint what you don't like about TV, so that your rules are not arbitrary. Is it what they watch or the amount of time they spend watching? If it is the quality of the TV programming, try the following:

- If you don't like commercials, allow PBS but limited commercial TV. Tape commercial programs and fast-forward through the commercials. Insist on your child learning to mute commercials when watching TV in "real time."

- If you don't like violence, do not allow violent cartoons or police programs. If you are concerned about sexism, adult themes, etc., do not allow music TV, TV after 8:30 pm, or any offensive program you identify. Teach your child the difference between news and sensationalism.

- Sit down with your kids and discuss the program while it's on. Don't spoil it for them, but do make observations to help them watch more critically.

3 If it's the amount of TV you are concerned about, select one of the following TV plans or come up with your own:

- No TV during the week. Allow one hour of TV news daily for the news-watchers in your family.

- Limited TV during the week. In the morning when kids are completely ready for school, they can watch until five minutes before it is time to leave. When homework is done, they can watch until dinner time. Other variations: allow special sports events, one classic movie, or one half-hour favorite program during the school week.

- Evening only TV. One half-hour each night. On heavy homework nights, videotape a favorite show for the next night or weekend. So that TV does not compete with bedtime, have kids wash, put on pj's and brush their teeth first. So, for an 8:30 bedtime, children should be in pj's and have teeth brushed by 7:30. They can then watch a half-hour show. At 8:00 it's time for a drink of water, story and goodnights, with lights out by 8:30.

- TV time trade. Your kids can earn TV-time by reading or doing creative projects or schoolwork. Try thirty minutes of TV per book read, or fifteen minutes for completing homework. Earnings can be cashed in on the weekend or daily when chores and schoolwork are done.

4 Don't keep the TV on as background noise; your children may become addicted to it and have a hard time turning it off their whole lives.

5 Don't be a TV junkie yourself. Your child will say, "It's not fair. You watch TV every night." TV can get in the way of a couple's personal life, reduce the benefit of family meals, and make the art of conversation extinct. Put a book by the bed. In fact, place it on top of the remote!

6 Introduce non-TV family activities. Your message should be "TV isn't important." Set up a card table for a jigsaw puzzle. Play games as a family. Read together. Get books and magazines from the library and leave them where your family hangs out. Who can resist a crossword or word search book (connect the dots or tic-tac-toe for younger folk) and a newly sharpened pencil?

7 Discover the radio. Wonderful news magazines are broadcast on National Public Radio and American Public Radio. Children's story hours, family music, variety shows, and talk radio can provide the whole family the opportunity to rediscover use of their ears and using "the mind's eye."

8 Have a Family Meeting to change TV viewing habits:

- State the problem: *"TV is interfering in our lives. We're fighting about the TV every day."*

- State how you feel about the problem: *"I'm so frustrated I want to give away the TV set."*

- Brainstorm solutions. *"I'm open for suggestions as to how we can watch TV less and use our time better."*

- Select a plan to try for a week that everyone can agree on (if the kids are uncooperative and have no plan, give a couple of plans which you consider reasonable).

- Have a follow-up meeting to see how the plan is going.

- Decide to keep the plan or adjust it to make it work better.

One family I know, formerly contenders for TV/Video Game Usage Champions of the World, had a Family Meeting and decided to move the TV to their father's office. In the evenings at home, family members now read (even the kids are reading the newspaper), play board games, use the computer, or just talk together. Homework is less of a struggle because there's no TV to compete with. If there is a special TV show everyone wants to watch or a video the family would like to rent, they have a TV pizza night at Dad's office. Getting rid of the TV created true quality time and the whole family seems more connected.

9 Try this experiment—put away the TV for one week. Then have a Family Meeting and note the differences in your lives. What was better? What was worse? Did you really miss anything? Do you want to adjust your TV viewing permanently?

10 Don't give a child a TV for her room. If, unfortunately, she already has one and TV watching is a problem, remove it.

11 Use an Announcement to prepare your child to turn off the TV. No one likes to be interrupted, but an Announcement can help:

Parent:	Cassie.
Child:	(eyes glued to set, barely hearing) Yah, Mom?
Parent:	Cassie, please look at me. (she looks at her mom)
Parent:	Thank you. In five minutes, it will be time to turn off the TV, and come set the table for dinner.
Child:	Okay.
Parent:	Thank you.
	(five minutes later) It's time to turn off the TV.
Child:	Mo-om. That was five minutes?

Parent: (calmly uses Broken Record). It's time to turn off the TV.

Child: Aw, Mom. A great show is coming on too. (Reaches for remote)

Parent: Thanks, honey.

SAYING NO and STICKING TO IT:

1 If she refuses to turn off the TV when you ask her to, present this Choice.

Choice followed by The PC—Perfect Child—Response:

Parent: You turn it off or I will, which do you choose?

Child: Darn. Why do I always have to turn it off? (goes to turn TV off)

Parent: Thank you.

More like reality:

Parent: You turn it off or I will, which do you choose?

Child: (silent)

Parent: You turn it off or I will, which do you choose?

Child: (refuses to choose)

Parent: Looks like you want me to choose.

Child: All right, all right. But I don't see why I have to. You watch TV whenever you want. (walks toward TV)

Parent: Thank you.

A child will prefer to turn the TV off herself, even under protest, rather than have you do it. And as it is never good to get into a physical conflict with your child, her turning it off eliminates the possibility of the two of you struggling over the remote.

This parent does not get detoured by her daughter's challenge, "You watch TV whenever you want." Whether it is true or not true is not the issue. You can discuss fairness later, after the TV is off.

If she does turn off the TV, praise her with a simple, but non-gloating, *"Thank you."* If she refuses to do it herself, you turn it off. No doubt she'll give you a tantrum of some sort.

2 If your child approaches you with a deal—*"I'll get dressed if I can do it in front on the TV"*—and you really want to compromise (you softy you)—I can't stop you. I would recommend, however, making a pretty tight contract.

> Child: I'll get dressed if you let me keep watching.
> Parent: You'll get all dressed? Even your shoes?
> Child: Yes. I promise.
> Parent: All right, let's try that. But if you aren't dressed
>   in 7 minutes, shoes too, the TV goes off. Agreed?
> Child: Right.
> Parent: You've got a deal.

If she get dressed, praise her. If she doesn't, turn off the TV. These kinds of deals can lead you right back to the morning struggle if you are too flexible.

3 If, when you turn off the TV, she throws herself on the floor kicking and screaming, (if she is not damaging herself or others) ignore her until she calms down. Turn away, remain in control, focus on something else. Walk, don't run, to make a phone call, wash some dishes, glance at the newspaper. The unspoken message to your child must be, "Your screaming isn't going to change my mind."

4 If she kicks the wall, bangs the door, or slams about the furniture, give a Warning of a Consequence: *"If you damage anything, you pay for it and no TV for twenty-four hours."*

She will no doubt try another slam or two, just short of doing damage. Ignore those face saving or testing efforts. If she escalates and does damage, immediately enforce the Consequence. (If you and your child frequently have bouts of this kind, seek out a behavioral specialist to give you one-on-one guidance.)

5 When, after the tantrum is over and the Consequence given, she "makes a small step in the right direction," tries to express her feelings in words, or uses a calm voice to negotiate a deal ("I promise to get dressed if I can watch TV"), you may respond to her in a positive manner. I'd not recommend you allowing the TV on, though, because you don't want to reward a tantrum.

> Child: (in a calmer voice) I promise I'll get dressed if you let me keep watching TV.
>
> Parent: I appreciate your promise, but you have lost TV for today. When you are dressed, why don't you read or draw until it's time for school.

6 Remember that a Consequence must be meaningful to the child and you must be able to follow through with it! Examples:
Turn off the TV now or no TV for the rest of today.

Turn off the TV now or you'll go to bed 15 minutes earlier.

Turn off the TV now or you will have a 10 minute Time-Out.

7 If, when you turn off the TV, she turns it back on, remove it from the house. Put it in the trunk of your car or garage. Before you bring it back, work out a deal for earning future TV usage.
If you will follow my TV rules today—
> *watch only one hour*
> *turn it off right after your show, and*
> *agree with your sister about the choice of program—*

then you will earn TV for tomorrow.

8 Praise your child when she follows TV rules and turns the TV off when you tell her to. *"I like the way you're cooperating now, thanks."*

9
Video Games and Other Toy Troubles

THE PROBLEM:

Your child begs for you to buy toys that you consider violent, addictive, dangerous, sexist, racist, or too expensive. You understand how hard it is for your child to want something that most of his friends have, but you wish he'd understand and accept your decision.

THINKING IT OVER:

This is another tricky one, because, once again, your feelings may be a bit mixed. Are video games too addictive, as well as being unncecessarily violent? Very possibly. If we forbid them, however, are we depriving our children of some skill yet-to-be-determined—but absolutely imperative—for their future succcess? Or are we setting up our children to be ostracized by their friends who do have video games?

What about toy guns? Do they promote aggression? Do gun-playing children become more violent than non-gun-players or is violence more complicated than the weapons themselves? Are squirt guns just good fun? The squirt guns that look like Uzi's—is that carrying water play a little too far?

With toys that seems dangerous, like in-line skates or skateboards, will a helmet, kneepads, wrists supports, and gloves make it safe enough? Should we just ignore our fears and trust our kids won't be harmed? Are we being overly protective if we say "no" to our child having these? Will we damage his relationships with peers if he's the only kid on the block not allowed to have a skateboard?

Does a Barbie player thinks less of herself than a non-Barbie player? Does Barbie's voluptuous frame destine our daughters to self-hatred? We know Native Americans and others are deeply offended by the portrayal of "cowboys and Indians," and that children's self-esteem can be adversely effected by negative cultural images. Toy manufacturers are coming out with all kinds of culturally diverse dolls and craft kits, but as a parent, I have a hard time telling what is an authentic and respectful portrayal from what would be a stereotypic, and possibly demeaning, portrayal.

If you are having a hard time setting limits on your child purchasing an item, it may be because you and your partner disagree on a toy policy. Your spouse may think, "What's the big deal about in-line skates? Just get him knee pads!"—however, you have seen the neighbor kid hobbling about on crutches following a skating catastrophe. Your partner may think there's a lot more danger in TV than in a Barbie. You are really not sure, but you'll ban both if necessary. You may feel that a particular video game system would turn your child into a zombie, but your partner wants to get one because he or she likes it! I can't help you too much here, other than urging you first clarify your own values, then negotiate a compromise with your partner as best you can.

When you talk together, look at the issues behind your gut impulse to say "no." Is there a way to address those particular issues? Is it possible to rent or borrow such a game system to see if you can regulate its use? If you have a video system already, can you be selective in your choice of games and set limits on the violence of the games and amount of time your child spends playing them? Is there a way to adequately protect your child when he's on skates or a skateboard by practicing on a playground until he is expert? Are there not attractive dolls which can bring as much enjoyment as the one with the torpedo chest?

Surely, if we completely deny our child an item, he may become obsessed with it. He may spend the next two weeks complaining, "But Jack has one!" and rushing off to Jack's whenever he has the chance. You may find you cannot stop the obsession, but buying the desired toy is not the solution.

My guess is that sometime or other in your child's life you will decide to deny a toy which he will proclaim he'll die without. When that time comes, use the following guidelines to help reach mutual understanding.

HOW TO AVOID BATTLES OVER TOYS:

1 One way to prepare for the toy wars is to anticipate problem situations. Watch your friends who have children a bit older than your child. What toy dilemmas have they faced or are they facing? Think about how you will want to handle the same challenges.

As you approach one of these situations, talk to other parents whom you respect. Have they said, "No video games" (or whatever you are concerned about) at their house? How do they feel about their decision? How have their children been affected? Do other kids hold it against them, or just accept that video games are not allowed?

Talk to parents who do not feel as you do, who do allow guns, video games, Barbies (or whatever). How has this affected their children? You might hear, "He played with it twenty-four hours a day for two weeks, then we never saw the thing again." Even some of the most addictive games may wind up abandoned in a corner of the bedroom. Your worry might be for nothing.

2 Clarify your values and establish the rules early. Of course, your child may or may not take on your values, even if he respects the rules.

My children learned as toddlers that Mom and Dad didn't allow guns. In spite of our no-guns rule, my son has always liked guns and wants to play with them if a friend happens to bring a couple over. I have seen him become bored with gun play, however, and talk his buddies into doing something else. If a friend leaves a gun at our house, Kyle may not even pick it up. It's impossible to know if Kyle has picked up our values or if he just has developed other interests.

3 As your child grows, discuss with him the images and messages given by the toys you are concerned about. Just as you can reduce the negative effects of television by watching it with your children, pointing out and challenging the images and messages presented, you can let your children know your concerns and values regarding the type of messages in the play they choose. You can note that Barbie's body shape is not a realistic one and that no one can look like Barbie without major surgical exports and imports. If your child must do battle, you can give him non-human monster types, rather than people figures. If you give children historical information about Native Americans, settlers, pirates, and soldiers, their imaginary play may have fewer stereotypes.

4 Avoid long-winded lectures. A few simple lines should be sufficient. Keep any further discussion on the subject short, sweet, and calm.

> *Your mother and I have thought for a long time about your having guns. We believe that killing is wrong, that shooting people is wrong, and even that playing at shooting is wrong. We have decided that you may not have guns and we hope you will understand.*

Remember the concept of neutrality. If you put a great deal of attention on something, it becomes more enticing, so go easy on the moral tirades.

5 As issues around toy purchasing come up during shopping trips, help your child get used to the idea that most of your trips to toy stores are for birthday or holiday presents for others. Prepare your child by announcing:

> *We're going to the toy store to buy Tony's birthday present. This is not a time to buy for you. You will see things you want but we will not buy them today.*

Also if Tony's parents are against, say Army figures, it's a great day for you. It always helps to have a buddy in the same boat.

Your son: Let's get Tony a GI Joe.

You: I know Tony wants one, but his mom asked me not to get him one. They don't like combat figures in their house either. His mom said Tony also likes music tapes and anything to do with bugs.

Your son: Cool Let's get him a bug cage.

You: Great idea.

Now we don't know for certain that Tony is not going to become a sadistic bug torturer, and we don't know for certain that all our valiant efforts are going to result in less aggressive children, but hey, we are here to make the best judgments we can.

6 Make sure you don't give a double message, saying on one hand, "You can buy anything you want with your allowance, after all it's yours" and "No Uzi water guns" on the other.

7 Rather than waiting for a confrontation in a toy store to deliver the bad news to your child that he can't have a video game system or she can't have a Barbie, have an open, honest discussion with your child at a calm time (bedtime is a great time to have a talk, but start early in the evening as it takes a while). Ask your child how she feels about the rule. Empathize with her without giving in on your decision (See Mirroring). You can start by saying something like, *"I know you are disappointed that we've decided not to have video games."*

You may be surprised at how accepting your child is of the decision, if you have explained it to her clearly once and do not waffle about it. You might hear her announce to a friend matter-of-factly, "We don't have Nintendo, but have you ever played Scrabble?"

8 If someone gives you the forbidden toy, you and your partner need to decide together what is the best course of action. I don't think giving it back is a good idea. I can't see what it will accomplish and it may embarrass friends or relatives.

You may decide you are just not comfortable, for example, having a gun, even if it is a toy gun, in the house. Sit down with your child and explain your reasons. Tell him you will return the item to the store and he can exchange it for something else.

If you decide the child may have the item, sit down with him anyway, share your reservations about it and delineate the guidelines for use. Say something like, *"Aunt Marge didn't know we don't allow guns and I do not want to hurt her feelings by giving it back. You may keep it, but we will have some rules about using it."*

When my dear friend Della wanted to give my daughter, Miranda a Barbie (which I did not want Miranda to have), I reluctantly agreed. Della's gift did not bring the end of the world. It did not curtail Miranda's passion for reading or stop her from wanting to be a doctor and, so far, at age twelve, she is neither boy crazy nor obsessed with the shape of her body. It would have been far more damaging I believe to take away a gift from a special "aunt."

When another friend, who was visiting from out of town, gave my son a particularly dangerous toy for his birthday, I kept from saying anything which would have embarrassed my son or our friend. Kyle had other presents to capture his interest so I put it up on a high shelf. We all forgot about it until this year. A toy which was inappropriate at age four is now terrific at age eight.

9 If your child seems particularly obsessed with images of violence and aggression, find constructive ways to channel his energy and impulses through active sports such as swimming and bike riding or karate. Also, set limits on the type of television programs and movies your child sees. There may be debate about whether they are harmful, but they can't be helpful.

SAYING NO and STICKING TO IT:

1 Don't say "no" until you have come to a firm decision and never set up a rule that you are not willing to stick to. If you give in to nagging and tantrums you will teach your child to nag and throw tantrums to get what he wants.

2 Your child may be quite accepting of your decision in the abstract. The tough time will come when you go to a store and face the tempting toy in the flesh, so to speak. Try these approaches:

- Remember the value of "redirection." Tell your child what he may have, rather than focus on what he may not have. In a store respond to the question, *"Mom, may I have Rollerblades?"* with *"You may have roller-skates."* Or to the demand, *"Dad, look at that neat gun! Can we buy it?"* reply, *"You may pick a game or a truck today."*

- Your child may have accepted your decision but that doesn't mean he likes it or will not offer some protest at some point, say in your trip to the toy store to get presents for his brother. When the asking/nagging starts, give a firm Command. In response to arguing repeat the message, using the Broken Record Technique, Warnings, and Consequences as necessary (See similar discussions of in-store behavior in Chapter 19, Grocery Store Begging and Chapter 21, Money).

Using the Broken Record:
(Parent repeats in response to all child's arguments)
We are only buying for your brother's birthday today.

Using Warning of a Consequence:
If you nag me any more, we will not stop for ice cream on the way home as we had planned.

Be sure and follow through if necessary

3 In general, do not lecture, explain or nag during a conflict about toys. Clear thinking is not possible during a tantrum. You'd be wasting your breath. Do, however, follow up later on in the day or evening with a brief explanation, clarifying to your child your values and concerns about the violence, the addictive quality, or the racist or sexist values attached to the toy they want.

10
Finicky Eating

THE PROBLEM:

Your child is a finicky eater. He refuses to eat what you serve the family, demands you cook him a special meal, or begs for a snack at bedtime. You find yourself giving him more junk food than you'd like because that's all he'll eat.

You want to be able to provide meals for your family that everyone will eat. And you'd like to prepare one meal in an evening, not a separate one for each finicky eater.

THINKING IT OVER:

Kids have major power over parents in the arena of food. Most cultures equate nurturing and comforting, namely mothering, with feeding. When our kids don't eat, we panic. Our concerns start early: panic when our newborn takes a week to learn to nurse, debating when to start our infant on solids, weighing veggie vs. non-veggie diets for our toddler, wondering if and when we should ever allow sweets and artificial foods, and finally questioning whether that our school-age kid is getting a nutritious diet when he only consumes burgers, pizza and macaroni.

I am announcing here and now that I take a hard-line position on indulging kids' eating whims; I'm totally against it.

You do not want to starve anyone in your family, but neither do you want your family's meals to be dictated solely by your child. Many people who enjoy cooking get discouraged when the menu is reduced to child-pleasers.

I recommend an eating plan that is simple, nutritious, shifts the responsibility for eating to the child, and keeps parents out of dangerous over-involvement that can result in eating disorders.

PROMOTING HEALTHY EATING:

1 Plan three meals a day for the family (your kids can help). Include something the cook wants to cook and a nutritious filling food such as pasta, rice, or potato for the more finicky eaters.

2 Also provide one or two snacks if you like, but make sure these are healthy foods such as fruits, fresh vegetables, or yogurt. The newest nutritional guidelines recommend diets going heavier on fruits, vegetables, whole grains and legumes, and lighter on dairy and proteins, with fats a small percentage of daily calories.

3 As a general rule, don't allow other snacking that will interfere with kids' appetites at meal times. If you want to allow some flexibility for the "grazing" types in your house, keep a bowl of fruit on the counter or a container of cut up vegetables in the fridge. A workable rule in many houses is "you may eat whenever you like if it's a food I'd happily serve at a meal" like an apple or a salad, whole-grained cereal or crackers, a hard boiled egg.

4 Avoid, as much as possible, fried, salted, sweet, and artificially colored and flavored foods. These are not only unhealthy, but they spoil your kid's taste for other foods. If they are filling up on potato chips and cola they will not be satisfied by the natural sweetness of fruit, the subtle flavor of vegetables, or the fragrance of herbs and spices. If you prefer they don't eat it, don't buy it.

5 Provide a clear expectation that everyone be home at mealtime and sit down together. If you have a chaotic schedule with all the adults working outside the home, try to eat together at least a couple of times a week. Some families have a regular Sunday dinner or brunch. Some find that breakfast is a perfect time to spend a few minutes together.

6 Other than compliments to the chef, don't let conversation center on the meal itself. Talk about the day's activities or what's ahead for the week. Certainly comment on a child who is eating well, willing to try something new, and so forth. Parents' praising one child often inspires another child:

(Franklin is gobbling up his peas)
Mom: You're certainly enjoying those peas, Franklin.
Ralph: Mom, I tried them. They aren't bad.
Mom: That's great you tried them, Ralph.

7 Serve your finicky eater small portions. A tablespoon or two may be sufficient. It will look more appealing and he can always ask for more.

8 Don't nag your kid to eat. Have a rule, *"You need to try everything once. If you don't like it, you won't have to eat more of it."* I have been continuously surprised by my children's response to trying something they thought they would hate: "Not bad" or "You can give me a little more of that."

Some families successfully use a "three bite" rule for foods kids are iffy about. This replaces the dangerous Clean Plate Club of the fifties. Don't force a child to eat three bites of a food that actually makes him gag, of course.

9 Never have the TV on during meals (except for an occasional pizza night with a movie).

10 Don't give up on a food forever, such as whole wheat bread or pasta, brown rice, or a certain vegetable. If your child pooh-poohs it, take it out of the repertoire and re-introduce it in a month or two. Children's tastes develop and change rapidly. My kids now surprise me by asking for and eating the very same foods that for months or years they refused to touch.

11 Think creatively. Make sandwiches with a slice each of white bread and whole grain. Slip a little spinach into an omelet or lasagna. Introduce bits of broccoli in a dish of pasta and parmesan, then increase the amount each time you serve the dish.

12 Don't overly indulge family members' contrasting tastes. Find ways to encourage everyone to eat the same meal. I have been driven nearly to distraction by my kids never liking the same foods at the same time. To encourage my son to eat spaghetti with marinara sauce (his sister's favorite), I started serving his spaghetti tossed in a tablespoon of sauce and then sprinkled heavily with parmesan. Over the last year I have slowly increased the amount of "red sauce." I was shocked last week that he asked for "extra sauce" as his sister always does.

SAYING NO and STICKING TO IT:

1 If your child makes negative comments like "This is yucky" or "Ick, this stinks," correct him once with:

> *Unkind comments about my cooking are not welcome at the table. If you would rather not have me serve this soup again, please tell me after dinner.*

2 After you have made the rule clear, ignore negative comments by changing the subject or distracting or giving attention to the child who is eating well or making appropriate conversation:

> Joey: I hate this.
> James: I like it.

Dad: Glad you like it, James. Hey, guys, tell me about soccer practice today.

Joey: Dad, may I have more fish?

James: How can you eat that stuff?

Dad: Sure, Joey, pass me your plate. Would you like more rice, too?

Certainly, if a kid keeps up the negative comments, you can give him the Consequence of leaving the table for a few minutes.

3 If your child won't eat, calmly say, *"You need to eat three bites,"* or *"I'd like you to try one bite."* It might help to give a Reminder, *"Remember, I'm not preparing any more meals tonight."* Then just ignore his not eating. Your basic guideline is "Don't battle over food."

Some kids respond to, *"If you want dessert tonight, you must have three bites of stew."* Yes, there is a danger in using sweets as a reward, but the greater danger is turning mealtime into a struggle. If you generally serve dessert, have a policy that dessert is a small treat which anyone gets if they have done a pretty good job eating. Don't, however, make dessert contingent on a clean plate.

4 No adult in the house should get up from the dinner table to cook for the pouting child who refuses to eat what's been prepared. For the child who demands other food you have two choices:

- Simply say, *"No."*

- Say, *"If you don't like what we're having, you may help yourself to fruit."* Or he can make himself scrambled eggs, carrot sticks, or cheese toast. Cereal might be fine too, but save sugar-laden breakfast cereals for dessert.

  I prefer the "no" approach, but if you prefer the "help yourself," that's fine. You also should expect that he will clean up any kitchen mess he makes.

5 If your child becomes rude or disruptive for any reason, he should leave the table for a short period of time. You may do this by giving a formal Time-Out or by saying, *"Go to your room. When you are ready to talk nicely (keep your feet to yourself, eat with your fork, chew with your mouth closed), come back to the table."* Of course, ignore any arguing.

6 If your child totally refuses to eat, abandon your rules regarding "try it once" or "three bites." Unless your child is having a sudden weight loss (in which case consult your physician), it is not dangerous for him not to eat a meal here or there. Remember, your role is to keep out of the battle.

Require only that your child sit at the table during meal time. Engage him in conversation as you would those who are eating. If he doesn't eat and chooses not to help himself, don't fix him anything else later. He won't starve in the night and most likely will have a great breakfast in the morning.

7 If, once you have your family on your three or five meal plan, your child is habitually not hungry at meal times, check out his habits. Look for signs of kids stopping for burgers on the way home from school, eating junk at a friend's house, or raiding months-old stashes of Halloween, Valentine's Day, Easter or birthday party candy from under the bed.

8 Don't be thrown from your course by the "I'm hungry" moans of a child at bedtime, usually accompanied by clutching around the navel area. More than likely this is a bedtime-delaying tactic. A good response is, *"Then you can have a nice big breakfast."*

9 If you are at all concerned that your child may have symptoms of anorexia (self-starvation) or bulimia (vomiting for weight control), or if you see a significant weight loss or gain (a sign of depression), see your physician immediately.

11
Sweets

PROBLEM:

Your child demands sweets, gum, sugary beverages, and desserts every night. She gets plenty, with all the holidays and birthday parties in life. You can't give in to every request for sugar or her teeth would fall out. Can't she accept no—even half the time—and be content, or at least quiet, about it?

THINKING IT OVER:

The world is full of tempting things not all that terrific for us. Sugar and butter-laden goodies are just part of the fare and, as you cannot leave the decision to your child, you and your partner once again get to volunteer as the bad guys, in an incarnation we'll call The Sweet Police.

Many families attempt to avoid introducing sweets until their children are exposed to them (at birthday parties, Halloween, Valentine's Day). This is not a bad plan and you can get away with it for a couple of years. Some parents will go to extraordinary lengths, bringing alternative food along to a party (raisins, crackers, yogurt) in hopes of assuaging their child's longing for cake and punch. Certainly when the child is old enough to realize she is getting a different "treat" than the rest of the party— including her mother who is swigging diet cola and licking fingerfulls of frosting—the double standard may do greater harm than a little portion-control would have.

You want to protect your child's teeth from early decay, keep her appetite for nutritious foods intact, and keep her sweet tooth undeveloped. You may not feel so bad about home-baked or "natural" sweets, but you might have strong feelings about chemical-laden "fruit drinks," overly preserved baked goods, sugar or sugar-free gum, and anything a color not found in nature.

No matter your philosophy on healthy and less-than-healthy foods, over and over you are going to confront the questions of how much, when, and what kind of sweet to permit, and, every so often, you are going to need to say "no" to sweets. The solution to this probably lies in that good old maxim "moderation in all things."

HOW TO KEEP SWEETS TO A MINIMUM:

1 The simplest way to cut down on sweets is not to have them in the house!

2 Watch your own sweet-eating habits. Kids do as we do, not as we say. I have a client who insists his kids eat healthy cereals, but he's addicted to the colorful sugar-coated crunchy ones. I've warned him, he's fighting a losing battle. (If you must have a double standard, eat your sweets out of sight.)

3 Have a clear eating plan (See Chapter 10, Finicky Eating). Three meals a day. A couple healthy snacks. Easy on fats, salts, and sugar. Easy on fast food. Sweet cravings are less of a health problem if they are a supplement to, rather than a substitution for, nutritious food.

Come to an agreement with your partner (so that you do not undermine each other) about the amount and type and frequency of sweets (gum, soft drinks, sugared/artificially colored cereals) you will allow. Find a middle ground if you have opposing positions on goodies.

Think moderation. You don't have to have dessert every night. We decreased our dessert evenings to twice a week, on Friday night at supper and at Sunday dinner. The kids have adapted and seem to appreciate the treat more.

4 Let your kids in on the rules about sweets and stick to them. Once your child knows and understands the rules, you can loosen them at parties, when a house guest brings a sweet for the kids, on the holidays, or when out to dinner.

5 Your child's behaviors and habits may shape your rules regarding sweets:

- You might consider tying sweets to good oral hygiene. If your child is a conscientious brusher and flosser and is getting good reports from the dentist—you may be more flexible.

- Take a cue from your child's tastes. My children Miranda and Kyle seem happy (for the moment) with junk in moderation (unlike their mother who is trying to learn from their example). At holiday time, when there is candy out, they usually ask before having any and a piece or two seems to satisfy them.

  For another child, a bowl of candy is too tempting. When Miranda's friend Abby is over, the holiday candy disappears in handfuls. Sweets are not allowed at Abby's house. Has the candy-ban created insatiable cravings for Abby? Possibly. Or it may be that Abby would have a sweet tooth in any family. If you have a child like Abby, help her out by keeping sweets out of sight.

- Keep healthy food snacks handy and in sight. A bowl of tangerines may keep your child from going on a cookie hunt or a reminder of cheese cubes in the fridge can ward off hunger and temptation.

- Help with Halloween. My dentist recommends that on this most difficult of all sweet-tempting nights, you surrender. Tell your kids they can eat all the trick-or-treat sweets they want, but that you will throw away the rest after bedtime. Children have a ball with this plan. They eat until they are sick of the sight of candy. And yes, they eventually stop. They become quite selective in their choosing, knowing they won't be able to eat all that night. When they are in bed, you throw away the rest of the candy per the agreement. (If this plan seems a little severe, have the children select one treat for the next day's dessert.) It will feel odd, throwing out perfectly good candy (an oxymoron?), but in November there will be no sticky bag of sugar under their beds tempting them day after day until the last grit-covered sour ball is consumed.

SAYING NO and STICKING TO IT:

1 If your child is asking for a treat and you decide the answer must be "no," give her a clear Command. Make eye contact, lean toward her, and say simply, *"No, honey, it's too close to dinnertime."* If she looks like she is going to accept your Command, say, *"Thank you for understanding."*

It's fine to tell her what she can have, *"There's carrots and celery or bread and peanut butter. You may have some of those."*

If she starts to fuss or beg, break eye contact immediately. If you are with others, turn calmly to them and engage in conversation. If alone, simply leave the room to attend to business elsewhere.

2 Remember, you can announce to her you are going to ignore:
*The answer is no. Raul and I are talking and I will not
listen to your fussing about this.*

Return your attention to your friend. Ignore her whining until it subsides. If she stops, but stays by you, you can smile or give her a small hug, or whisper, *"Thank you,"* as you continue with your conversation.

3 If she gives a full blown tantrum, on the floor screaming and flailing about, you have three choices:

- My personal favorite—completely ignore the tantrum until it subsides. You will win the victory of Establishing Parental Credibility and actually reduce the possibility of future major tantrums. Engage in conversation as if your life depended on it. Keep a smile on your face and talk through your teeth to your friends. Beg them, *"Help me through this, ignoring is not my strong suit!"* Or say, *"Let me show you my plants (etchings, cobwebs, whatever),"* and lead your friend to another room.

- Offer a When/Then Deal:
  When you can talk to me quietly, then I will listen.

  Turn back to your conversation at this point and ignore until she gets under control and can "use her words" rather than her volume.

- Give Warning of a Consequence:
  If you continue screaming, I will give you a Time-Out.

  Of course if she doesn't stop in a short time, you must give the Time-Out.

4 Praise your child as soon as she stops nagging or screaming about the gum, or whatever, goes to play, changes the subject, or starts another behavior you like.

Family Matters

Everyone in the family matters. Every one counts. The hard part about every one counting is that frequently some one in the family doesn't get what he wants when he wants it. A hard lesson for the little guy, sure, but one to teach well before he becomes a teenager.

12
Swearing

THE PROBLEM:

Your child swears, curses, or uses silly bathroom language. He picks just the right words to get you going or embarrass you to tears. Whether at home, in the market, or in front of Grandmother, out comes the bad language and you are furious. You can't believe your child would show such disrespect.

THINKING IT OVER:

Language is a big issue for most parents. Kids can push a lot of buttons with their choice of words. Most parents, no matter how permissive, relaxed, or liberal, have a limit when it comes to the type of language they will tolerate.

Children may use bad language for a variety of reasons, but I think most of the time it boils down to three: get attention, show exasperation, or on occasion, to be deliberately mean (as in name-calling). These are a lot easier to address than the spicy verbal habits of adolescents, who pepper their chat with foul words because that's what their friends do, or who use words as weapons of fury directly against their parents.

I think children use bad language because they hear it (from family members or other kids), try it out, and discover it inspires a powerful reaction in their parents. Like with other bad habits, they keep trying to get that powerful negative parental reaction.

Dealing with bad language is a two-part process: 1) come to agreement with your partner about what language you will accept and what language you will not accept, and 2) use a limit-setting plan to stop the bad language when it occurs.

HEADING IT OFF AT THE PASS:

1 Watch your own language! Children do as we do and not as we say. Believe me, there is no compromise on this one. Because I have trouble in the Bad Language arena, myself, I tried to introduce the idea that using bad language, like driving a car, having a drink, or being up until midnight, was a grown-up privilege which my kids could have when they turned twenty-one or left home, whichever came first. It may have been great logic, but it didn't produce the habits I was aiming for. I had to resort to cleaning up my language.

2 Make it clear that some words are not acceptable. Explain they hurt feelings, cause embarrassment, are disrespectful, profane, vulgar, racist or sexist, and will not be tolerated.

3 Avoid getting bent out of shape by the early bathroom words. Your best defense with toddlers is to ignore. They have already sensed the quick reaction they can get with the "Poo-poo, pee-pee" and so forth. You can use a simple Announcement of ignoring with your child:

> *My ears don't hear silly words like that. They just stop working.*

Turn away and pick up a newspaper and ignore the few more words you can expect to follow before he gives up altogether.

4 When the school-age child tests out bad language in your home, you may try ignoring at first. Truly it is possible to stop much bad language with ignoring. In fact, I believe the combination of ignoring bad language at home and setting limits on it in public is the fastest way to stop it altogether. The reason ignoring works for two to twelve-year-olds is that much of the time they are using bad language to get our negative reaction. If we don't react, they have less reason to swear. Remember, kids don't usually swear alone.

5 Do have some language allowed for moments of frustration. My son stopped himself from swearing by first switching to swear words in German. I am not sure where he got the translation, but it was a lot easier to bear.

For a while my family relied on nonsense words, inspired by Roald Dahl's *The BFG* (Big Friendly Giant), a marvelous book for every one in your family. We'd hear from various corners of the house, "Oh, fleeble-squash!"

6 Praise your child for using appropriate words. If, in a moment of frustration, you hear him choose acceptable words, thank him. If his language has been particularly bad until this point, you might want to give him a small reward.

7 Don't take kids' bad language personally. The older child might pick up language from his friends and try it out at home. If you overreact, he may increase its use. Give a simple, calm reminder, *"Greg, I'd rather not hear that in the house."* Who knows? You may just hear, "Okay, Mom."

8 Take the power out: say the bad words yourself. Let's say your kid drops something on his foot. He shouts, "Shit." You calmly respond with, *"Sorry you hurt your foot, honey, but please don't say 'shit' when I'm around."*

9 Use a Better Behavior Chart. Have one item "Uses good language with one Reminder" along with several other items, at least three of which are easy for your child to achieve.

Give your child a sticker when he has used only good words throughout the day (the Reminder allows one slip of the tongue). Leave the space blank if he forgets. Praise the successes. Ignore the failures.

You can tie the stickers to a reward which he can collect on the weekend. If each day's sticker is worth one point, for example, throughout the week, every time he has earned six points he can have a treat from the Treasure Box (See Glossary).

SAYING NO and STICKING TO IT:

1 If bad language continues, in spite of your more positive or low-key approaches, you may just have to resort to using a Consequence. It is most effective to use a Warning before giving the Consequence, so that your child clearly knows what to expect. The Warning acts as a reminder. Your child knows what's coming and has a good chance to practice self-restraint. A Consequence is the removal of a privilege:

- which has meaning for your child

- over which you have control

- which you are willing to take away

- and is which is minimal.

Some families find that fining a child twenty-five cents per word is a quick, effective Consequence. A Time-Out will work well in public. And, as always, removing part of TV time or play time can be highly effective too.

2 Never, never, never wash your child's mouth out with soap. I do occasionally hear parents claim it works, but it hardly is a "minimal" Consequence.

13

"But Everyone Else Can"

(Hanging Out at the Mall
and Other Horrors)

THE PROBLEM:

Your child insists on being allowed to do something which you think he should not do (because it's dangerous or because your child is too young, for example) and his complaint is "But all my friends can." He wants to ride his bike on busy streets, stay out after dark, go to the movies with a friend, or leave the school playground to visit a fast food joint.

You want your child to be safe and you want him to respect the rules. He doesn't have to like them, but he needs to follow them. You'd rather not have a major confrontation every week on the subject.

THINKING IT OVER:

Every parent faces the dilemma, how to protect yet not overprotect, how to balance keeping your child safe against his real need for increasing independence and opportunities to learn responsibility.

The baby learning to walk needs you to let go of his hand and risk tumbling. He won't learn to walk if you insist on holding onto him all the time. Likewise, at four a child needs to begin to explore life beyond his yard, a child of ten needs to explore the neighborhood, a child of fourteen needs to explore his community.

These are not always safe environments. Each parent must use his or her best judgment as opportunities for letting go arise. Your child will want the least restrictive option and may tantrum in response to your "no," but in the end you must set rules which make you feel comfortable. When you set those rules, your child will not like it, but he will know (somewhere below consciousness) you do so because his safety is of utmost importance to you.

Be careful of being a "knee-jerk no" parent. Every time your child requests such an opportunity for independence, explore it carefully. Assess the worries that lurk behind your immediate impulse to say "no." Explore your options. Is there a middle ground? A way you can say "yes" without putting your child at risk?

Likewise, if you tend to be a "knee-jerk yes" parent (quite likely the son or daughter of a "knee-jerk no" parent) or a parent who wants to say "no" but wants at all cost to avoid confrontation (or who feels you cannot control your child and that he'll do what he wants anyway), keep in mind that your responsibility as a parent is to keep your child safe. The world is a far too dangerous place these days, and your limits are essential to protect your child. And although kids won't admit it, often they are quite relieved when you set limits.

Keep in mind that your parental task is to give your child increasing independence so that by high school graduation he will feel ready to leave home for college, training, or career. He has a long way to go and you help by providing opportunities for small, safe steps.

HOW TO GET YOUR CHILD TO RESPECT THE RULES—(when other kids don't have them!):

1 When your child presents his request—let's say he wants to hang out at the mall with a group of friends—ask him what he thinks about the idea. Sometimes children ask to do things because other kids urge, "Go ask your Mom!" You just might find he is very uncomfortable with the plan and is more than relieved when you say, "No."

2 If he clearly wants the privilege and you are hesitant to allow it, talk it over with your partner. If you feel clueless as to what is appropriate and safe these days, check with the parents of your child's friends or slightly older neighbor children to see how they would handle or did handle the situation.

Consider some options your child would like that are safe. In the case of the mall example, the parent might be willing to accompany the child to the mall but would shop or window-shop separately from the child and his friends. Perhaps the boys could attend a movie or use their allowance in the arcade for an hour, with everyone synchronizing watches and meeting at a pre-designated spot.

Come to a decision with your partner about whether the answer should be "yes" or "no" or "under these conditions."

3 Present your decision to your child. If he accepts it, praise him: *"I appreciate your understanding and accepting my decision."* (If he doesn't, read further.)

4 Let him know under what conditions, he can have the privilege, for example:

Your dad and I are comfortable with dropping you guys at the movie while I do a few errands at the mall. I'll meet you when it's over. It's not being on your own totally, but it's a start.

If you want to go with Jason's big brother, that would be okay with us because he is eighteen and a very responsible kid.

5 Attempt to be fair and consistent, weigh each decision separately, and take into consideration your child's ongoing maturation. Think "small steps toward greater responsibility." At age six, kids can sit at their own table in a fast food restaurant. At age eight, they might be comfortable in the pet store while you are in the card shop next door. At ten they might be safe in the book or game shop for a half hour or more (safety depends upon where you live, of course). At age twelve they possibly can attend a movie with a parent dropping off and picking up after the movie.

If your child sees that as he grows he earns more privileges, he may sense that "all things come to those who wait" and will trust that you will be granting more and more freedom.

If, in this loosening of parental reins, your child does not handle the new privilege well (is not at the designated spot at pick-up time, is picked up by the security folk for unruly behavior, etc.), then he should lose the privilege for a period of time, for say two months. This is not to be overly punitive, but to postpone the privilege until he has matured a bit more. Then, with very clear expectations and clear Consequences laid out, he can try again.

SAYING NO and STICKING TO IT:

1 You can't prevent his frustration and disappointment at your "no," but you can deliver the bad news with empathy (See glossary for Mirroring). Sit down with your child and tell him your conclusion. Try to put yourself in his shoes and let him know you understand his feelings:

> *I've thought seriously about your wanting to hang out at the mall with your buddies and I've decided that it's not safe enough. I'm sorry. I know some of your friends have permission and that you'd really like to be able to go with them. You probably think I'm being ridiculously overprotective or that I don't trust you.*

Avoid lecturing. Briefly present the concerns you have, but don't belabor them. Your child knows half your arguments already and won't want to hear the fine details. He'll be too angry or hurt to weigh the information and should be allowed to nurse it a bit. Later on in the day or the week you can have another talk about it if you want, but in the midst of your telling him "no" he's not going to be particularly receptive to your wisdom.

2   If he argues or uses back talk at your decision and explanation, repeat your message using the Broken Record Technique.

Dad:	The subject is closed. (picks up the newspaper and begins to read)
Son:	(shouting) You're being unfair! Why can't I go?
Dad:	The subject is closed.
Son:	Why can't I? Don can! Max can! Even Tim can!
Dad:	(not arguing) The subject is closed.
Son:	Call their parents! They'll tell you its safe. There are all these grownups around. What—you think somebody is going to shoot me at the mall?
Dad:	The subject is closed.
Son:	Is that all you can say! (mimicking) The subject is closed. The subject is closed.
Dad:	(turns the page of his newspaper and reads)

3   If he starts to yell or curse, tell him you're going to ignore: *I'm not going to respond to stomping, screaming and badgering. If you have some information you'd like me to consider, write it down. In an hour I will look at it. For now the subject is closed.*

4   If he has a full blown tantrum, continue to ignore. This will take great strength on your part. You may have to leave the room. Do it calmly so it won't appear that has succeeded in driving you away. Your demeanor must indicate that you merely have something to else to do: get the newspaper (great for ignoring), use the bathroom (you're only human), check to see if you left the stove on (is that gas I smell?), return a phone call (to someone who won't mind a little background noise).

5 If he goes out of control, give him a Warning of a Consequence:

The subject is closed. If you continue to scream and bang doors, you will be grounded for the evening.

6 If he sneaks out with his friends, breaking the rule you have established, you must give a Consequence. The Consequence should be the removal of a privilege, which is important to him and that you have control over. It should be given immediately and be for a short period of time, longer for the older child. In our example, the Consequence might be that he loses outdoor play for the rest of the day, is grounded for Saturday, or restricted from play with his "partners in crime" for the weekend.

7 If your child persists in breaking important rules meant for his safety, consider consulting a therapist who specializes in behavioral parent training.

14
Things That Make Parents Uncomfortable

(Sleepovers, Walking to school, PG-13 movies, Baby-sitting, or Other Stuff)

THE PROBLEM:

Your child asks permission to do something about which you are uncomfortable, like going to a slumber party when you don't know the family, walking (and crossing busy streets) to school, going to a movie which you consider too adult (scary, sad, sexual, violent), or baby-sitting alone at night. You would like your child to understand as far as she is able and to accept your "no," even though you might be basing your decision more on instinct than reason.

Unlike the privileges described in Chapter 13 "But Everyone Else Can!" these are less clear for you. You are inclined to say "yes," except you have a nagging, underlying hesitation, more of an instinct than a well-developed rationale, and you wonder if you are being overly and unnecessarily cautious.

THINKING IT OVER:

Sometimes we don't have clear or concise reasons why we want to deny our child a privilege. We just have a discomfort about something they want to do. Our hazy reasons seem silly when we try to articulate them.

Sometimes parents don't quite trust their impulses because they were raised by parents who were overly permissive or overly strict. They might fear repeating the pattern of their parents or rebelling so ferociously that they err in the other direction.

If you have doubts about a particular privilege and your reaction to your child's asking for it, seek out the wisdom of parents you trust or your child's teacher.

Certainly you and your partner don't want to set limits arbitrarily, and your child will be more inclined to accept your decision if she can understand reasons for it, so do attempt to articulate your worries. If finally it comes down to "I just don't feel comfortable about it," use the following plan for telling your child.

HELPING YOUR CHILD UNDERSTAND AND ACCEPT YOUR "NO":

1 As your child grows, attempt in your dealings to be open, honest and fair with her. Try to have well thought-out reasons for the rules you set, to follow them consistently, and to apply them equally to all children, taking into consideration their individual temperaments when safety is concerned.

2 When she comes to you for permission, get the whole story from your child and clarify with her exactly what privilege she is asking for. Find out what her true feelings are on the subject. Sometimes kids ask us for permission before they have really decided if they want permission or not. She may be hoping that you will say "no" and get her off the hook.

3 Give yourself some thinking space by saying, *"I'd like to think about your request. Let's talk in an hour."* (Or the next day, if she'll wait that long!) It is okay for you to take the time you need. If she balks a little at that you might say, *"I'm leaning toward saying 'no', but if you give me some time to think about it, there's an outside chance I'll change my mind."*

4 Take that time to separate your emotional response (your knee-jerk response) from the real facts about safety. Identify your issues of concern. Try to find out exactly what makes you uncomfortable about her request.

5 If your child is asking for a privilege that most of her friends have, you may want to seek out the advice of other parents at this point, to check out if you are being unnecessarily cautious. Of course, you might or might not want to follow their example. Some parents are overly permissive, provide too little supervision, tend to spoil their children, or give in to nagging too frequently. In the end you must rely on your gut feeling.

6 Because you are feeling a bit torn about this decision, I think it is fine to entertain her appeals if she makes them calmly and courteously. There's always a chance she'll add information or suggest other arrangements which will make a difference in your decision. For example, you might allow her to:

- Baby-sit, if she finds a next-door neighbor who is going to be home to act as emergency backup;

- See a PG-13 or R movie, if you see it first and find it's appropriate;

- Walk to elementary school, if she finds a fourteen-year-old who walks that way to junior high;

- Stay overnight at someone's house, if she arranges for you to meet the friend and her parents in advance.

SAYING NO and STICKING TO IT:

1 If you come to a final conclusion that you are uncomfortable with her request, let her know and tell her why as best you can. For example, tell her that your primary concern is for her safety and that is the basis of your decision. Let her know at what age and or under what circumstances you feel you will be able to give her the privilege she wants.

2   Your child may keep asking or attempt to argue, explain or make a deal with you. She has a right to differ with you, but you have a right to make a final decision and have discussion on the subject come to an end.

3   If she keeps arguing at this point, use the Broken Record Technique. Simply repeat a phrase such as, *"I've made my decision and the discussion is over,"* until she gets the message.

4   Ignore all tantrums, stomping off, slamming her door, rolling her eyes, mumbling under her breath, swearing, or whatever else she does to express her anger. She doesn't have to like the decision, only abide by it.

5   At bedtime, or another quiet time, perhaps you can talk it out and help her come to some peace about it. Give an example from your childhood, if you can recall one, when your parents made a decision which you later understood was for the best.

6   If she should sneak out and do what you have decided she may not, you will need to follow up with a Consequence. Your child needs to respect your rule, not matter how she feels about it and no matter how torn you were about making it!

15
The Wrong Clothes

THE PROBLEM:

Your child demands to dress in a manner you consider to be inappropriate. She wants to:

wear dressy clothes for a casual occasion

wear play clothes for a dressy occasion

wear sneakers to a party

wear party shoes to the sandbox

wear shredded blue jeans anywhere

go out jacketless in the cold

go out shoeless in the wet

You'd like your child to wear what you selected for the occasion or a reasonable alternative.

THINKING IT OVER:

Kids have few areas in which they have control. They may not be able to control their environment, but they have some power when it comes to their own bodies. It is no wonder that children battle with parents over eating, hair styles, and clothing selection (witness adolescent anorexia and creative, if not outrageous, hair and clothing choices). Certainly, allowing children flexibility in choosing their clothing is a relatively harmless way to give them a little power in a world where they have none.

Choices in clothing often reflect family values or patterns. Some parents are comfortable allowing their children to choose their play clothes only, feeling that school or church demands more conservative ("respectful") clothing than their child might choose. Others provide choices for their child within some limits (clothing should match, be clean, be neat, not be torn, etc.) Some parents are comfortable with giving free rein in clothing matters.

One issue to consider is your level of embarrassment. You may feel you will not be considered good parents if your child's dress does not meet certain standards. You might ask yourself if your child's attire is more important to you than it need be, because you are concerned with how it reflects upon you. A teacher friend voiced the concern that some children try so hard to look good at school that they wind up looking too good; they overdress and separate themselves from their classmates.

As children grow, their friends and classmates influence their choices for the good or bad. What is absolutely essential attire to your child may be out of the question for you! By adolescence you may have to give up anything more than a little advice—and only when asked! But for the below twelve set, you can usually prevail on important clothing matters.

All this said and done, however, in every family's life there are times to set a standard for your child to follow. And every now and then, there will be some event, some occasion—party, funeral, or just the lousy weather—when you and she will be at odds.

HOW TO GET YOUR CHILD TO DRESS APPROPRIATELY:

1 Set some family clothing rules, for example, that clothes must be clean and weather-appropriate, and that on certain special occasions special clothes will be necessary. Beyond those rules, leave as much as you can up to your child.

Think about it. Do you really care what your nine-year-old chooses for the slumber party, your three-year-old chooses for the playground, your six-year-old chooses to wear over to his friend's house, or your eleven-year-old wears out for hamburgers? Hold the line at dirt and indecency.

2 Try inviting cooperation before you get to a head-on collision. Use Announcements, Choices and the When/Then Deal.

An Announcement, a few days in advance of the occasion, gives your child some time to accept your decision:

On Sunday, we will be going to Grandma's. I'd like you to wear the dress she gave you.

A Choice gives your child a little flexibility, but has an underlying message "you need to pick one or the other":

For Grandma's birthday you may wear the green jumper she gave you or your blue party dress. Which do you choose?

A When/Then (or If/Then) Deal offers an incentive (a privilege) for cooperating with you:

If you will agree to wear the dress Nana gave you, I will get you a new hair ribbon to go with it.

3 For the preteen, try the "What's Your Plan?" approach. When you ask your child about her plan, mention the issues which concern you and that you'd like her to consider.

I'll want you to look really nice for your Aunt's birthday party on Saturday. What were you thinking of wearing?

Asking her rather than telling her conveys that you trust she will choose wisely. She may rise to the occasion with a great suggestion or ask you to make the selection.

SAYING NO and STICKING TO IT:

1 Think through your position before you give your first "no." If your decision is a rational one, based on pretty good reasons, and you're committed to it, then stick to your decision. You needn't explain over and over or put up with all kinds of arguments. As I have said before, it is not helpful to your child when you give in to a tantrum. It only teaches her that a tantrum will get her what she wants.

2 Make sure your child knows why you have made the decision. Choose a couple of sentences to clarify it for her:

Your shoes are brand new. We must save them for special occasions.

Your sneakers are dirty; they are fine for the playground, but not for temple.

I want you to be dressed up to visit Nana. It shows our respect for her.

For play you may dress as you like, but for school I expect your clothes to match.

It's raining. You just got over a cold. I want you to wear a sweatshirt or jacket.

3 Acknowledge your child's wishes using the Mirroring technique, but make it clear you have made a final decision:

I know you want to wear your dressy shoes. They are very pretty and I know you want to show your friends, but they will be ruined at recess. Then you won't have them for parties. Wear your sneakers, please.

I understand you really want to wear your play clothes to Nana's. But this is Nana's birthday and we are all dressing up for the party.

4 If she presents (in a relatively calm manner) a good reason for you to change your plan, certainly consider it. We're all capable of making hasty decisions and often benefit from added information. If she presents a plan to wear her good shoes to class and bring sneakers in a bag for recess, you might not mind so much.

Likewise, you might entertain the possibility she could bring play clothes to her grandmother's house to change into later on.

5 To combat arguing, use the Broken Record Technique: keep repeating your message. Example:

Parent:	I want you to wear your sneakers to school.
Child:	They are so uncool.
Parent:	Wear your sneakers to school.
Child:	I'll be careful. Really I will. I won't wreck them.
Parent:	Wear your sneakers to school.
Child:	You're so unfair.
Parent:	Wear your sneakers to school.
Child:	Will you stop saying that?
Parent:	Wear your sneakers to school.
Child:	Okay. I'll (mimics you) wear my sneakers!
Parent:	Thank you.

6 Follow through on your decision. Do not allow your child out of the house in the new shoes, the dirty sneakers, without the jacket, or in the "wrong clothes." Avoid any physical battle, certainly. Instead give a Warning of a Consequence.

If you don't take off your dressy shoes, you may not go to the playground.

If you don't put on your boots, you may not play outside.

If you do not take off the ripped jeans and put on some slacks, you will not come with us to the movie.

If you do not change into one of your two good dresses for Grandpa's birthday dinner, we will cancel the overnight with Kelly tomorrow.

Be sure to follow through with the Consequence if she refuses to cooperate.

7   And, of course, ignore sighs, rolled eyes, mumbling under the breath, name-calling or back talk. Calmly turn away and turn your focus to something else. If she stamps off to change to the appropriate clothing, say a simple, *"Thank you."*

8   Always praise when she goes along with your clothing plan. *"I appreciate your cooperation."*

16
Pets

(When You Just Can't Have One)

THE PROBLEM:

Your child will not cease begging for a pet. You barely can take care of your child, your job and your life, never mind something that makes messes, yowls, begs, whimpers, has fleas, dirt, fur, and probably will need a funeral someday.

THINKING IT OVER:

This is a tough one. Pets are wonderful for children. Pets teach them how to care for others, to think about the needs of others, to shoulder responsibility, to handle commitments. Pets provide marvelous companionship, play, or comfort. And while some pets are large and require lots of maintenance, others are small and barely tax you at all.

But not all of our living arrangements allow for pets. You may not have the space or yard. Your landlord may not allow pets in your building. A family member or roommate may be allergic to animals. Your family may be gone from home most of the day or travel frequently and you seriously may doubt the critter would be happy or well cared for. Perhaps you truly do not have the time or energy to care for one more living thing. (If the plants are wilting, how will an animal survive?)

You may have these or other good reasons for not getting a pet, and my guess is you're reading this because you want to—or need to—say "no," and are pretty close to doing so. You can't prevent your child from disappointment, but you can help him accept disappointment by being understanding.

HOW TO SAY NO TO GETTING A PET IN THE LEAST PAINFUL MANNER POSSIBLE:

1 If you've not yet said "no," and there's still a possibility you'll reconsider (Sorry, but I am the single mother of two children, a dog, a cat, and a few plants!)—take the time you need to think through your feelings about it. Say to your child, *"I'll have to think about that,"* and do so.

During the thinking-it-through process, don't let your child badger you into a premature "yes." That is not good for either of you. You lose Parent Credibility and badgering will become his major tool of negotiation. Get back to your child with the answer and stick to that decision unless circumstances change. Your child's nagging and tantrums should never lead to your giving in to something you truly do not want.

2 Consider having a Family Meeting to discuss pet pro's and con's. However, in a Family Meeting you will be at a disadvantage. Your children will promise the world. "We'll feed it, we'll bathe it, we'll walk it, we'll clean its cage, we'll scoop its poop." And the tricky part is that they will mean it. They truly envision themselves happily enslaved to their new best friend. And you may be tempted by their vows. So, on your con list put, "I don't want to have to remind you to feed it, etc."

A possible outcome of a Family Meeting is to downgrade the type of pet. They wanted a dog, you'll settle for a small well-caged rodent. I warn you against anything that requires exotic or live food however. Your children will no doubt discover they need food for Snuffy the Snake (who eats only tiny white mice from the tiny white mice farm thirty miles away) on Sunday night (true story). And no matter the good intentions the kids have, you're the one who drives, right?

3 Use this format for the Family Meeting:

- State the problem: *"You kids want a pet. We grownups don't want a pet."*

- Identify the issues behind the problem.
  Mom and dad's issues:
  The mess, the reminding, the fleas.
  Kids' issues:
  The fun, the friendship, just how neat it will be.

- Brainstorm solutions (Write them down).
  No pet.
  Smaller, hairless pet.
  A single-celled ameoba pet.
  Self-feeding tube or dish.
  Keeping pet outside.
  More frequent visits to a relative who has a pet.
  Borrowing a pet for a weekend to try it out.
  Kids pet-sit for neighbors during their vacation and see how they handle the responsibility.
  Regular visits to a pet store or zoo.

- Pick one solution you and your children are willing to try.

- Agree to conditions. (This is tough. What do you do if it doesn't work out? Give it away? Plead with the store to take the little cutey back?)

- Have a follow-up meeting to assess the success of the solution you picked. Adjust the plan as necessary.

SAYING NO and STICKING TO IT:

1 BUT I'VE DECIDED I CAN'T HAVE A PET!!! THIS IS A BOOK ON SAYING "NO," ISN'T IT? Yes. You may say "no" (As I did twice last summer to two sets of stranded kittens). Your family is not a democracy. It is a benevolent monarchy. Sit down with your child and say, *"I've thought carefully about having a pet and I'm afraid I have to say 'no' right now."*

It is fine to commiserate with your child about this. You can learn to be a good commiserator with a feedback technique called Mirroring. This may not fix the situation for the child, but at least he will get to state his case and be heard. Being heard and understood is very important to us all.

Such a talk might sound something like this:

Meg: I want a kitty sooooo bad.

Dad: Sounds like you really wanted a kitty.

Meg: I do. I really really really really want one. Please, Daddy?

Dad: I know how much you really want a kitty. And I wish we would have one, but we can't.

Meg: Daddy, pleeeeease.

Dad: You're very disappointed, aren't you?

Meg: Yes. (Starts to cry)

Dad: I see how sad you are. I wish I could fix it, but I can't.
(Crying continues)

Dad: You wish I could fix it, too.

Meg: (Nods) It's not fair. Everybody else has a pet.

Dad: I bet it seems like everyone in the whole world has a pet, but you.

Meg: (Sniffles) All my friends do.

Dad: All your friends....Well, sweetheart, I really hope we will be able to have a pet someday, but it's not the right time now.

Meg: But when can we, Daddy?

Dad: I don't know. A pretty long time I guess.

Although this dad really wants to "fix it," he can't. He makes a good choice: rather than trying to ease the hurt with reasoning or advice—neither of which will be soothing—he is truthful. He doesn't deny the feelings or try to cheer up his child before she is ready. He simply allows his child's disappointment.

Mirroring may not stop the discussion about a pet and you may have to commiserate a time or two more. Just listen again and let the child know you understand his feelings.

2   If your child has disappointments that aren't easily soothed, try these wonderful ways to help a little:

- Keep a journal. Give a diary or blank book to your older child and suggest that he write in it about his feelings. With a child who can't write or can't write as fast as his thoughts come, take on the role of "the pencil." Tell your child, *"I am the pencil. You tell the words to me and I'll write them down. I won't say anything. I won't disagree or get mad or laugh."* Your child will come to treasure his diary, finding it a welcome ear for troubles. You'll see him re-reading it or even sharing it with friends.

- Make a feelings "book." For toddlers, make a picture book of a few pages. For an "I want a kitty" book, draw a sad-faced child and draw a kitty. Then make a picture of you and your child or whatever pictures your child wants (even a preschool child can make his own pictures).

  Now ask the child to tell the story. Print the words under the pictures. Staple the pages together. Make other books as your child has emotional or physical hurts, anticipates changes in his life, or needs to soothe the greater traumas of separation, divorce, or death of a loved one (or pet).

3 If major nagging occurs, you may have to resort to ignoring. Remember to announce that you're going to ignore: *"Look, honey, I know you want a pet, but as I've told you, we cannot have a pet now. I'm not going to listen to any more fuss about it."*

4 If there is more fuss, simply ignore completely or repeat: *"The answer is 'no.'"* Or *"The answer is still 'no.'"* Keep calm, focus on a newspaper, and ignore until your child stops the fussing. As always, when he stops fussing and starts a behavior you like, be sure to give him some form of positive attention.

"Thanks for understanding we can't have a pet right now."

5 Do not, I repeat, do not give in to nagging, threats, screaming, stomping, arguing or other badgering. The worse thing you could do after you've made your decision to give in. Repeat to yourself, "I have the right to say 'no.'"

17
Music, Music, Music

THE PROBLEM:

Your child is not a teenager yet, but the music is blaring. It comes from a radio, boom box, tape, or CD, and it comes out louder than you can stand. You want peace and quiet, particularly quiet.

THINKING IT OVER:

You were a kid. You played music. You played it too loud. You drove your parents crazy. What goes around comes around. Maybe you just buy ear plugs, wave a white flag, and retreat to your room.

Your little kids like music, but music becomes life's blood for your soon-to-be teens. It brings kids together, gives them a common frame of reference, provides the glue for their social life, and helps them establish an identify apart from their parents. As important as music is to kids, however, they will not die if their parents set a limit or two around its use and abuse.

I don't want to talk about music content necessarily. I think that censorship of music is a very personal decision. I, myself, am not so hung up on the words, but that may be because I can't understand them anyway. (Was that my mother talking?) As for images, I do not allow music television on in my house because of the preponderance of sexist and violent visual messages (unless I watch it with them and provide a clear editorial voice-over).

Content aside, the next issue is noise and intrusion on others. Like the use of the telephone, the goal is to balance the interests of all people living in the home. Do kids want and need music? Yes, they do. Do you have a right to a reasonable decibel level? Yes, you do.

RADIO FREE HOME-LIFE? Not Exactly:

1 Start a counter offensive when your kids are little by introducing them to your favorite music. I'm an old Motown freak. For years I've gotten away with dictating the car and kitchen radio fare. My kids got hooked and we now croon in unison. It won't last forever, but it's given me a couple of years.

2 Model respecting the audio rights of others. Your kids will learn from you. If the TV is too loud for someone, turn it down. If the talk radio in the kitchen is too loud for someone, turn it down. If the grownups' music is too loud for the kids, turn it down. If any body's noise is too loud for the neighbors, turn it down. Not off necessarily, down. It's a reasonable request and deserves a reasonable response.

3 Allow your kids some free music time where they can happily play their music as loud as the speakers will bear and jump around to their hearts' content. Get a great book, some ear plugs and camp in the most remote corner of your home. If they get some free music time, they will be able to handle some music-free time. Let's hope anyway.

You can even set it up: *"Hey, guys, if you want to dance in the living room and play your music, that's cool. But after eight o'clock I'll be in there reading the paper and will need it quiet."*

4 For audio protection, invest in a set of headphones. One set per kid might be even wiser. If either the volume or the type of music gets too much for you, announce, *"Time for headphones, guys."* You may need to monitor the volume a bit to protect ear drums.

Figure out the best level by listening yourself (assume your ears are damaged from your early days and be conservative) and mark the dial to indicate the volume limit. Occasionally check to see if your kids are keeping the volume in the safety zone.

5   In the car, I think it's only fair that the driver has final say about the volume and kind of music played. Driving requires concentration and some of us are easily enough distracted by the road. On long trips, invest in headsets, books on tape, or music all can agree on. Or change family disc jockeys every half-hour, inserting a half-hour of silence or just chat every so often. (See Car Fighting, Chapter 2.)

6   Sometimes it's not the volume, it's the bass. Show your kids how to adjust it, so your home stays on its foundation.

7   Make it clear—music can't interfere with homework. Some kids can study well with music in the background, but if your child is dancing rather than working, use the When/Then Deal:

When your homework is done and in the backpack, then
you can turn on your music.

If your child can concentrate and complete her work with her music on, that's a great talent for a budding teenager, but she should try to learn how to study without music, too. She is going to need to be able to study in quiet places, so that she can tolerate the silence of the classroom or library. As many adults have found out, it is all too easy to become dependent upon TV or music as background noise.

SAYING NO and STICKING TO IT:

1   If the homework rule or the volume rule is broken, feel free to take The Final Recourse; unplug the machine or confiscate the batteries. There is no reason for you to have to endure something that drives you or other family members crazy and there is no reason music should take precedence (even though it may for our children) over homework.

2 Ditto for chores. Some kids turn on their tunes and turn off their brains. If, when the music is on, you can't get them to stop for a few moments to listen to you or feed the cat or set the table, just turn the darn stuff off until the chores are done.

3 Let's check to see if turning off the music fits the criteria for an effective Consequence:

- Does it have meaning for your child?
  Yes, yes, yes.

- Do you have control over it?
  If your child lets you turn it off and keep it off, you have control. If he doesn't, you can establish control by moving the player to the garage.

- Are you willing to use this as a Consequence?
  Absolutely—in fact the danger is being too willing!

- Is it minimal?
  If it's for a short time, a few minutes to an hour.

Turning off the music appears to be an effective Consequence. Remember to first give a Warning, then be willing to follow through. Here is an example of a Command, followed by a Warning, and finally a Consequence:

(Loud music. You enter. You can't get eye contact, much less ear contact. You wave wildly. You give a "T" sign for time-out. Someone turns down the amplifier a bit. You give a Command.)

You: Hey, kids, after this cut, I need you in the kitchen to set the table.

Kids: Aw, Mom. Do we hafta?

(You ignore that remark and leave, confident your loving children will do as you have asked. Two songs later, you return, turn down the music, give your Warning, and leave.)

> You: Guys. That cut was long over. I'll give you thirty seconds to show up in the kitchen ready to work, or the music goes off for the rest of the night.

(Most kids will head to the kitchen at this point, but for some reason your kids ignore you. You enter a third time, turn off the amplifier—unplug it for the drama of it if you like—and say:)

> You: No music until tomorrow. Dinner will be ready in ten minutes. Set the table now.

4 If you start to feel guilty during any of this, remember the concept of Benign Monarchy. Repeat your Monarchic Mantra:

Who pays the rent (mortgage)?
I pay the rent (mortgage).
Who runs the house?
I run the house.
The jobs won't get done if I don't do them.
The kids won't move if I don't nag them.
Who's the Bad Guy?
I'm the Bad Guy.
It's a lonely job
and it's mine.

Make up your own Mantra. Whatever works.

5 If the whole music thing gets out of hand, have a Family Meeting. Use these steps:

• Before the meeting, define the problem.
The music is a problem. No, actually the problem is the kids are ignoring me when they have their music on. I'm sick of nagging about chores and homework. I'm sick of having to scream to be heard.

- Think of possible solutions.
  Throw away the tape player.
  Hide the tape player.
  Have a rule; no music until chores and homework are done.
  Ban music except on the weekends.

- Reassign chores again and insist on follow-through. If they're not done, no music until the next day.

- Plan a meeting time and sit down with the family.

- Stay cool, calm, and firm.

- State the problem to the family: *"When you guys play your music, you ignore me when I ask you to do your chores."*

- Ask for solutions: *"I have a couple of solutions in mind, but I'd like to hear your ideas."*

- If no one is in a problem-solving mode, announce your pre-determined solution: *"Since there are no incoming suggestions, I have one— music only on weekends."*

- This might inspire some input. Allow everyone to Brainstorm and throw out suggestions. One family member can write them down. Don't comment on their merit, just record them.

- Eliminate the solutions anyone finds objectionable ("You can't throw out the tape player, Dad.") and cross them off the list.

- Look at the ones you have not crossed out and agree on one solution to try.

- Set a follow-up meeting to assess how the plan is working. If it is, congratulate everyone. If it is not, try another solution from the list.

6 Don't expect your kids to curb music on their own. They have no motivation to do it. You (and possibly the neighbors) are the only one who is suffering here, the only one who is interested in change. Loud music? It works for them.

Too Much

"Less is more."
— *Browning*

"Moderation in all things."
— *Terence*

"'Tis enough and 'twill serve."
— *Shakespeare*

"Enough is enough."
— *anon*

"The Answer is NO."
— *Whitham*

18
Demanding Designer Clothes

THE PROBLEM:

Your child demands the designer jeans or expensive athletic shoes that "everyone is wearing." The jeans she begged for a few months ago, she now dismisses as not "cool," "hot," "rad," "hip" (whatever) and definitely the wrong shade of blue. Not to be outdone by his sister, your son refuses to be seen in a pair of perfectly decent athletic shoes that overnight have become "gross." You'd been planning to buy another pair just like them because they'd worn so well! You want your child to select clothes within your budget. You are tired of the sulking, eye-rolling, sighing, and most of all the lack of gratitude!

THINKING IT OVER:

Once upon a time you pictured shopping trips as opportunities to bond with your growing youngster, but they have become the bane of your existence. No one likes to deny their child's desires, but $75.00 for a pair of jeans and $150.00 for sneakers! Please.

We remember from our childhood how nasty and critical "friends" can be to each other about such superficialities as clothing. We want to save our children from the cruelty peers can inflict, but we also want them to see that it is their friends who are off-base here, that life is not a fashion show. We hope to help them practice better values than their peers and have enough confidence in themselves to stand up to ridicule.

I have met parents who have indulged in designer-buying but then get discouraged by how carelessly their kids treat these expensive items. Even if you can afford to be extravagant, you are not necessarily doing your child a favor by giving him whatever he wants. At some time in life he will be supporting himself and will benefit from your lessons on value, quality, and realistic spending.

This is a tough issue—but you will solve it by talking with your child before or after, not during, the trip to the store.

HOW NOT TO BATTLE OVER CLOTHES— AND STAY WITHIN A BUDGET:

1 Arm your child against peer pressure. Prepare him for a time when he might not fit in with the crowd. Celebrate when he makes a brave choice that goes against the crowd or takes a risk. This groundwork may not seem to have much to do with choices in clothing. It has much to do with building character, which helps children stand up for themselves, their ideas, and their choices, including clothing.

Read books to your child that have underdog or unusual heroes, that celebrate emotional bravery and inner strength. Talk with your librarian to help you choose such books for children at any age.

When your child comes home with reports of other children being teased or picked on because of their physical, social, racial, religious, or other differences, use these as important learning times. Ask your child to put himself in the shoes of the child being teased. What was he feeling? What about the bully or bullies? Why did they pick on their classmate? What did your child feel watching it? What did he do? What did he want to do?

2 As your child grows let him in on some of the realities of shopping. It's okay to say, *"We can't afford that right now,"* or

"That's too much to pay for this, let's wait until a sale," or *"This is not well made and not worth the price."* Save up for the item by buying it on layaway (delayed gratification—a useful concept to introduce at this age). You will set a good example of choosing wisely and being a careful shopper.

3 Shop together so you can pick clothes you both like. Parents often shop for their children by themselves, but soon after age eight if not before, this becomes impossible. You and your pre-teen will have contrasting tastes unless you are extraordinarily lucky.

4 Before the shopping trip (before he has found the two hundred dollar jacket) discuss with your child what he thinks he needs and what you are thinking:

Example:

> *We can go to the mall this weekend to get the jacket you need. I have a budget of———dollars to spend. If you think you are going to want to spend more than that, you may use your savings. How does that sound?*

5 If he finds an item that makes you shudder at the expense, think through your options: pay for the darned thing, say "no," share the expense, or find a compromise. Have some solutions and a "bottom line" in mind (the most you are willing to contribute for the item in question).

6 Give your child a Choice rather than cajole him into buying something he won't wear. Let's take, for example, a daughter who insists on buying a certain brand of expensive jeans. Her mother might tell her:

> *We can afford two pair of reasonably priced jeans or one pair of designer jeans. We won't be able to buy more jeans for six months. If you agree to wash them and not wear them dirty, you may have the more expensive pair.*

Who knows? This child may choose two pair of the lesser price. Or she may buy them and take marvelous care of the over-priced pants. We learn best from experience after all, not our parents' well-meaning lectures.

7 Listen to the concerns of your child. They may seem trivial, but they are very important to him. In fact, I believe your understanding of the peer pressure he faces may be more important to him than actually getting the item he wants. A talk with your child might go something like this:

Parent: Tell me about these sneakers you want so badly.

Chris: I just have to have them. They are so cool.

Parent: They sure look terrific, but they are very expensive—and you know how quickly sneakers wear out.

Chris: But all the guys are getting them.

Parent: I see. This is the kind everyone wants and you think that they'll all be able to afford them.

Chris: Sure, Kevin has them already and James said his parents will buy them for him.

Parent: They cost much more than we can spend. You could have two pairs for the price of one of those. But they do look really like great sports shoes.

Chris: They are really great for basketball. I could jump twice as high in those shoes, I'm sure.

Parent: I bet you could. But what about the last pair of shoes you got? You seemed to like them and they lasted a long time.

Chris: Dad, nobody wears those anymore.

Parent: Oh, those are "out" now.

Chris: Only real nerds wear those.

Parent: So it would be pretty embarrassing to wear that style.

This example shows that even though the parent has not given a firm "yes" or "no," he and his son are talking in a civil manner. The dad is doing his best to see the situation from his son's point of view (called Mirroring). This father could now successfully try problem-solving using the Family Meeting format:

- State the problem.

- Identify the issues behind the problem.

- Brainstorm solutions; actually write them down.

- Pick one you are both willing to try.

- Have a follow-up Family Meeting to assess the success of the solution you picked. Adjust the plan as necessary.

Parent: I would say that the problem is you would like to have me buy you athletic shoes that cost twice as much as the shoes I can afford to buy you, but that these shoes are very important to you. Do you think I've stated it fairly?

Chris: Sure.

Parent: Let's look at the issues behind this problem. What are our concerns?

Chris: That they cost too much.

Parent: Good. That's one of my issues. And another of my issues is how quickly shoes wear out and how quickly feet grow.

Chris: Well, I can't help that.

Parent: And what are your issues?

Chris: If I wear anything else I'll look like a jerk.

Parent: And your friends will think you look like a jerk.

Chris: Right.

Parent: Anything else? No? Okay, I think we've got the issues figured out, now to the possible solutions. Let's make a list of everything we can possibly

	think of to try. But the rule is nobody can criticize anyone's suggestion.
Chris:	My solution is: you buy me the shoes.
Parent:	Another is for you to get a pair for————dollars or less.
Chris:	I can't think of anything else.
Parent:	You could pay for them yourself.
Chris:	Oh, sure—where would I get that much—
Parent:	Remember, no criticizing yet!
Chris:	Maybe we could try to find them on sale.
Parent:	Now you're thinking!
Chris:	Or I could go barefoot the rest of my life.
Parent:	Or we could split the cost.
Chris:	What do you mean?
Parent:	Well, I could put up the amount of money that I believe is fair and you could pay for the rest out of your savings or allowance.
Chris:	Or you could pay for them all and I could pay you back, by doing chores.
Parent:	We have a bunch of ideas written down here. Let's each put a check mark by the ones we would be willing to try.

In this meeting the parent and child are actually thinking up some workable solutions. They need to select one and iron out details: the amount the dad will pay, the amount the son will pay, the re-payment schedule if the son is to earn his share. They also need to address the other issues which the dad brought up, such as the shoes wearing out fast. Perhaps the son will agree to take care of the shoes and accept certain Consequences if he does not.

If you do choose to buy an expensive item because you can afford it, it is a special occasion, or you are splitting the cost with your child, it is fine to establish some conditions, for example: *"I don't want to see these sneakers left outside, worn untied, or covered with mud—if so, you will finance the next pair."*

SAYING NO and STICKING TO IT:

1 If you are unable to come to a compromise and your child will not agree to any of the solutions you have discussed, you may just have to put your foot down and cancel the shopping trip.

2 If your child starts in with a pre-adolescent repertoire of raising his voice, sighing loudly, rolling his eyes, slamming around, cursing under his breath, cursing over his breath, whining, moaning that his whole life will be ruined, or stomping about the house, don't give in. You may be moved—that's what the dramatics are designed to do—but don't give in!

3 If you must say something, tell him once, and once only, that his carrying on is not going to change your mind. In a calm, controlled manner say: *"I understand you are upset. If you talk about it in a quiet voice or write me a letter, I'll be happy to listen, but for today the trip is canceled."* Then turn away, pick up a magazine, make a phone call, look to see what's in the refrigerator, and wait until he talks to you in a reasonable voice.

4 If you are in a store and he creates a scene, give a Warning of a Consequence. *"If you cannot speak in a normal voice, we will leave the store now without buying any shoes."* For this Consequence to have weight, you must truly be willing to leave the store without the purchase. And if he continues to yell, you must turn and walk away calmly and confidently toward the exit of the store. Walk deliberately to the car (don't run—he needs to be able to follow you) and get in. Occupy yourself with reading road maps or the car registration until he has buckled his seatbelt, then start the car and drive home.

Do not take your child shopping again until you have had a Family Meeting and arrived at a shopping plan.

5 For toddlers and young children who tantrum during a shopping trip, the Consequence can be that you leave the store and that the next trip they stay home. On that solo trip certainly take into consideration their current tastes ("yes" to lavender and pink, "no" to turtlenecks or collars, "yes" to zippers, "no" to buttons, "yes" to sweat pants, "no" to jeans), but make your decisions based on your best judgment.

6 Praise your child, no matter how angry you still feel, when he is willing to sit down and talk rationally about the situation, comes up with a workable plan, accepts the reality of the budget, or solves his dilemma in a creative way. For example, one child I know, announced to her mother right before a special dance at school, "Susie and I are going to switch—I'm going to wear her best dress and she's going to wear mine."

Her mom's response was very positive: *"What a terrific idea! And with some of the money we'll save, how about if I take you girls to get your hair done."*

19
Grocery Store Begging

THE PROBLEM:

In stores, particularly grocery stores, your child cannot walk by the candy counter or toy rack without demanding you buy her something. She whines or pleads for sugar cereals, chocolate, gum, a small plastic something; she simulates cardiac arrest when you refuse. You? You want a nag-free grocery trip. Simple as that.

THINKING IT OVER:

If children asked once in a while for a treat at the market and accepted our "no" almost as readily as our "yes," I don't think this would be much of a problem. Parents get frustrated when asking becomes begging and when their firm but pleasant, "No, not today, sweetheart," results in screams.

First of all, what actually bugs you about your child's in-store begging? Is it what she begs for? Or that she begs at all? If she is begging for food, is she actually hungry? Would a healthy snack before shopping or buying her a yogurt solve the begging problem? Or is it that your child would beg even if she had just eaten a three-course meal and had her pockets filled with trinkets?

For your older child who may bargain with "I'll pay for it myself!" you are forced to consider exactly why you don't want to buy the item. You don't want her wasting her money? You don't want her to have candy or soft drinks? You hate the cheap plastic litter that is accumulating in her room?

In the end you have three choices: 1) to decide that shopping is never (or rarely) treat time; 2) to let your child spend—waste?—her own money; or 3) to give up and give in to the demand for a food snack or a coin for the tiny toy machine. I would recommend the first; I hate grocery store begging that much. Certainly you may do the second; friends tell me that if kids must pay for their own market treats, treats become less crucial fast. And, of course, you may go with the latter; some families find that a reward at the end of shopping inspires fantastic cooperation. A warning however: if you reward frequently with goodies, rather than with your praise or attention, your child will come to expect and demand these rewards every time.

"Reward! Never!" you may think, "Don't I have a right to cooperation on these trips without resorting to bribery? I'm not just shopping for myself, I'm shopping for the family." True, these are not personal pleasure trips and yes, you do have a right to run this all-too-frequent errand with minimal stress and unnecessary expense. Praise is a welcome reward in and of itself for terrific store behavior. Once the no-begging rule is clear, an occasional treat will be fine—and, in fact, truly a treat.

Whichever you choose, decide on a treat policy before you get into the market, not after you've entered that tempting place.

HOW TO GET A NAG-FREE SHOPPING TRIP:

1 Clearly establish the rule: *"No asking for treats and toys when we shop."* (If you are shopping and your child is hungry, buy a healthy snack of fruit, nuts, or rice cakes.)

2 Honor that rule. It is fine to be flexible, but it's confusing and unfair if rules change too frequently. If you decide to reward your child one afternoon, for example, by allowing her to buy a toy because she did extra chores for you earlier in the day, make it clear, before you enter the store, that the special treat is for the extra chores she did. Wait a while before you allow a shopping trip treat as a reward again, so that she does not come to expect it or beg for it.

3 As you enter the grocery give your child a brief Reminder. (Don't lecture!). *"Remember, Lisa, no asking for presents in the grocery store. The answer will be 'no.'"*

4 After the first few minutes of cooperating, praise your child. *"Lisa, you are doing a great job helping me shop,"* or *"Thank you for remembering the rule, Lisa."*

5 Give her specific shopping tasks, constructive ways of getting your attention. Hold up two cans of tomatoes and let her pick the one to buy. Give her the choice among several cereals or have her select the number of oranges you need. She can count each potato as she drops it into the bag you are holding. Ask her advice in making such decisions as, *"The curly pasta or the wagon wheel pasta?"* Let your older child do some of the shopping. Depending on her age, give her one, two, or three items to retrieve. Tell her the number of the aisle you will be on or have her meet you in the fruits and vegetable area in a couple of minutes.

As you involve your child, she will get lots of attention from you, and eventually will understand why you are purchasing what you are purchasing and why you say "no" to certain items. It's not that you are a selfish, mean mom or dad, but that you have a shopping plan and are working within a budget.

Sometimes you will not be able to take time to involve her. When you are in a hurry let her know in advance that you will be making the choices. Tell her what she can do to help this trip. Say, *"Today we are in a big hurry. I will pick out the food, but you can help me push the cart."*

6 If every jury in the land would find you guilty of Giving In to Begging and you would like to ease into a better habit, try substituting the If/Then variation on the When/Then Deal. On your way to the store, offer a "prize" for good cooperation to be given when you get home, for example:

If you don't nag for treats in the store, right after we get home, I'll play a game with you.

If you don't beg for treats in the store, you can choose from the Treasure Box when we get back.

The Treasure Box can have rolled up pieces of paper with activities that she likes to do written on them.

This Deal will be helpful in weaning your child from the expectation that treats will be bought in the store. In a couple of visits you can substitute verbal thanks for the more tangible treasure.

7 One family I know has a "toy-a-month" policy. They allow each child to purchase one very inexpensive toy or treat every month. When they are in the grocery or doing other shopping and their child wants a trinket they simply say, "Is this your toy for the month?" The child then contemplates whether they really want that toy or want to hold out for something better. The family reports this reduces begging on all shopping trips.

SAYING NO and STICKING TO IT:

1 In the car or outside the store, give a Reminder about the rule: *"Remember, no asking for treats when we shop."*

2 If your child starts to beg or fuss, tell her you're going to ignore her begging: *"I said, 'No candy' and I'm not going to talk about it any more."* In a second or two redirect her attention by asking her which apples or bananas look best.

3 If your child gives a full blown tantrum, ignore as if your life depended upon it. Pretend that noisy character is not your child. Walk a few feet down the aisle, but not so far that you scare her or appear to be running away from her. Read all the labels you find in eyeshot. Comment to curious onlookers, *"Kids! It's always something, isn't it?"* Or if you are willing to admit parenthood, say *"That book I read said to ignore—not as easy as it sounds!"*

Wait her out, staying calm no matter what she does. It will take only two or three successful bouts of ignoring for your child to get the message that Mom and Dad don't give in to screaming, that when Mom and Dad say "no candy" they mean "no candy" and no amount of screaming will reap candy.

4 Keep helpful thoughts in mind:
I can outlast her. I can outlast her.
This could be my last major in-store ignoring battle.
I survived labor; I can survive a tantrum!

5 Be ready to praise. You never know when she will snap out of her tantrum. It gets pretty boring when no one is reacting. When she calms down, give some form of positive attention, like involving her again in the shopping. *"Oh, no, we forgot dog food. Poor Custer! Help me find some."* (Ignoring is not effective unless it is followed by positive attention.)

6 If she's a toddler, and it's time to leave, give her a Choice: *"We're leaving now. Do you want to walk or shall I carry you?"* If she falls to the floor in a display of fury, say, "Looks like you want to walk," and walk directly, slowly, and confidently (hah!) toward the door. Make sure she can see you and that you know exactly where she is. Don't make eye contact. Stop and check out the charcoal or plants on display. It may take a while, but eventually she will get on her feet and follow you, half-heartedly, of course.

When she catches up to you, give a neutral Invitation Back to the Family, such as, "Do you think Mommy will like that raisin bread we picked out?" If she barks, "No!" at you, just ignore it and try again in a few minutes. As long as she is doing what you want, you can tolerate the lingering negative attitude. Your child needs to save a little face here and will not want to reward you with cheer.

If she indicates her Choice is to be carried by saying (or screaming), "Carry me!" you can say pleasantly (but not triumphantly), "I'd be happy to carry you." Stretch out your arms, sweep her up and say "Good Choice." Again, just ignore her grumpiness.

7 If giving the Choice to walk or be carried doesn't work, and she remains in a screaming heap on the floor, give a Warning of a Consequence that is important to her. For example, if you were planning to go by the pet store to look at the new kittens, you could say: *"If you don't come with me right now, we won't have time to look at the kitties at the pet store."* Give her a moment or two—check to see if your keys are in your pocket—and then start to move toward the door. Most likely she will follow you, though reluctantly.

Be careful not to reward a tantrum. Only withdraw a privilege you have already planned and which the child knows about. If the dad above had not already announced the kitty-visit, he shouldn't use it as a Consequence. The child would get the message: "If I tantrum, Dad will promise to take me to the pet store to get me to stop."

You may have to just pick her up kicking and screaming. Do it calmly but firmly, turning your face away to avoid hits or scratches.

8 Do not lecture, explain or nag. Clear thinking is not possible during a tantrum. You'd be wasting your breath.

9 When, on this trip or another one, she gets off the floor and joins on her own accord, praise her with a simple *"Thank you."*

20
"Just One More!"

THE PROBLEM:

Your child demands "one more" time down the slide, video before bed, game at the arcade, ride on the bike, cookie from the jar, game or bedtime story, or demands its ever popular cousin "just five more minutes." You'd like not to have to turn into the Bad Guy after having a fun time with your kid.

THINKING IT OVER:

Kids don't want fun to end. They are never ready for parents to say "It's time to go," or "That's it, no more." It's impossible to be Hero or Heroine at transition-from-play time. The kids have had control over their lives for a while and we are wresting it from them.

We try to give clear messages and set firm limits and let's face it, sometimes our hearts aren't in it. We holler, "Ten minutes, guys," and we mean somewhere between five and thirty and the kids sense it. And because we're not totally committed—a little nagging, a little whining, a little begging, and we're putty. So, what's the harm? "One more" won't really hurt, will it?

Some parents are not bothered by requests for "just one more." They experience their kids as being reasonable. They consider the situation, sometimes say "yes," sometimes say "no," the kids accept the decision and that's that. But if your child never accepts your "It's time to go," read on. The remedy is simple, really.

HOW TO GET A CLEAN GETAWAY:

1 Establish a pattern that you can follow consistently. Your pattern may include:

- An Announcement of how many more minutes or how many more times (as in "down the slide three more times,").

- An "It's Time to Go," statement when that time is up.

- A Rapid Getaway.

2 Know Thyself. If you are likely to allow "one more," why not just give the privilege up front. *"You may have two cookies"* is better than giving one and then a second after she bugs you for it.

Likewise, giving the Announcement, *"You have ten minutes more at the video machine,"* is better than telling your child that it is time to leave and then giving in to begging for two "five minutes more." The main idea here is: don't reward nagging.

3 Be ready to go. If you give your Announcement, telling your child it is time to go, but then spend twenty minutes saying your good-byes, you'll lose credibility. She'll ignore your message, "It's time to go," because she knows it's not.

4 Once you have mastered sticking to your guns, and your child consistently will take "no" for an answer without anything more than an "Awww, Mom," you can experiment with being flexible.

You may respond to non-whiny reasonable requests or "new information" (i.e., "Remember, Mom, there's no school tomorrow. How about ten more minutes?").

You may accept an offer of a Deal if you are sure your child will follow through. My kids might bargain, "Can't we stay just ten minutes longer? We promise to get up right away in the morning." That's a pretty good deal for me. If ten minutes can buy me a morning of cooperation I might be persuaded. But if the next morning is a struggle, I'll not be accepting many deals in the future.

SAYING NO and STICKING TO IT:

1 Prepare yourself for the situation you are dreading by deciding what you want and the Command you are going to give in order to get it. Let's take the example of leaving a friend's house. You give an Announcement, *"We'll be going in five minutes."* The five minutes is up and you say, *"We're leaving now."* Of course, you have already organized your things and said your good-byes, so you head toward the door or exit. Your actions should support the message, "We're leaving now."

2 Don't give in to any of her many possible tactics: begging, nagging, whining, crying, pleading, cajoling, or a sudden coughing fit. Keep to your task, leaving. Open the door, hold it for her, and wait calmly. Your demeanor should say, "There is no 'more' and I will wait here all day until you figure it out."

3 If your child throws herself on the ground, ignore it. Break eye contact and turn away slightly. Or you may proceed deliberately and calmly as long as it is safe. Don't leave a small child in the house alone as she might panic. (If you are at a park, walk only a few feet away from a child and make sure you can see her out of the corner of your eye.)

4 If she does not follow you and she is small enough, you may have to carry her out. Do so as calmly as you can. Turn your face away from her. Think, "Firm and neutral, firm and neutral." Ignore the screams and protests. Ignore the "I hate you's."

5 If your child actively defies you give a Warning of a Consequence. For this to be effective, the Consequence must be the removal of a privilege:

- Which has meaning for your child

- Over which you have control

- Which you are willing to follow-through on and

- Which is minimal, (short, immediate).

Consequences which work for families include:

- Earlier bedtime by 15 minutes.

- Loss of an electronic privilege (TV, radio, video game).

- Loss of use of favorite toy child uses daily such as skateboard, bicycle, skates, train set.

- Loss of extra (not only) bedtime story or shortening (not eliminating) of the bedtime ritual (talking time, lullaby).

In the case of a child who has run back to hide in another room, the parent might follow the child, get eye contact (or "ear contact" if she is out of sight) and give the Warning in a serious, firm tone: *"Come with me now or there will be no TV tonight."* Turn and walk away. Your child may take up to a minute to follow. If she does not come within a reasonable period of time, follow through with the Consequence.

If your child earns a Consequence once or twice, she will learn you mean business when you say, "It's time to go now."

6 Be consistent. Hang tough. Each time you assert yourself and stick to your decision, it will give you strength for the next encounter. I promise you it will get easier.

21
Money

THE PROBLEM:

Your child demands money for toys or other goodies. You want your child to use his allowance, earnings, or savings instead of nagging you for money. You'd like him to accept that he can't always have what he wants when he wants it.

THINKING IT OVER:

Families want their children to understand the value of money, to know it doesn't grow on trees, and to learn about earning, saving, and spending money wisely. To that end they may give an allowance or allow their child to buy a toy in exchange for doing chores. Parents have a hard time, though, with in-public asking (or begging) for money. On the spot, surrounded by strangers, parents are tempted to give in, rather than risk a scene.

If expense is not the issue parents might think, "Why shouldn't he have it—I can afford it," or "I get pleasure from giving to him, why not give?" But even when you can afford it, a nagging voice inside says, "I shouldn't just give whenever he asks, should I?" I think that's a good voice to listen to.

There are several reasons to be judicious in doling out presents and money. Most of us remember from our childhood that toys we earned ourselves held special value for us. We perhaps know an overindulged child, who has the unattractive habit of expecting handouts on a regular basis and an insensitivity to the limits of the family pocketbook. We occasionally observe our own child quickly forgetting about toys and doodads he got without any effort; they wind up on the floor of the bedroom or are left lying about in the car or outdoors.

Maybe it seems that every time you are out with your child he asks for money to spend, so that he turns errand-running or window shopping into a nightmare. Perhaps he is a terrific saver, stashes every penny, and has more cash on hand than you do. Yet he won't spend his money; he wants to spend yours!

Think about the values you want to instill in your child, then establish policies in your home about random treats, parental loans, cash on demand, and other financial possibilities.

TEACHING MONEY MANAGEMENT (Money Sense Not Nonsense):

1 In general, avoid giving frequent handouts. Children develop better values and appreciate money and toys more if they are earned, saved for, or given on special occasions.

2 Give an allowance. Allowance can be tied to chores or given just because the child is part of the family and needs to have a little income. Ask other parents the going rate, but use your best judgment and keep it very reasonable.

Give allowance regularly and give it on time. Too many parents neglect to have the cash on hand or forget about payday altogether. If we want our kids to be responsible, we need to be responsible in our dealings with them.

3 Open a savings account for your child at your bank. He can learn about saving and earning, and interest, too.

4 Work with your child on budgeting. If he wants to run to the local store to spend all his allowance on junk, tell him some things he could purchase with two or three weeks' savings.

Having "free" spending money on an outing can teach a valuable lesson. On vacation my daughter spent all her spending money in a few days by visiting the "penny" candy store and going out for burgers with friends when home cooking didn't seem exciting enough. Toward the end of our trip, we went to a bookstore, where her brother still had money to spend. She had none. "Boy, I learned my lesson," she announced. And I didn't even have to lecture!

5 If he runs out of allowance, let your child earn money by doing special chores. Regular chores get old. Sometimes kids cheerfully do jobs just because they are novel. My kids hate to empty the dishwasher, but occasionally find sweeping the front stairs or mopping the kitchen floor a novelty. When they are in a money-earning mood, we negotiate mutually pleasing agreements.

6 Establish a "wish list" for your child for birthday, holiday or special occasions. When he asks for something say, "What a great toy to put on your wish list."

7 In general, watch out for commercials. I established a rule when my kids were young that I would not buy toys which they saw on TV (and nagged me about). Consequently they never begged me for TV merchandise. I got a respite during the holidays.

8 As your child is growing, establish clear and specific expectations about store behavior. Do the Trial Run to achieve smooth errand running:

- Have a less-than-crucial errand in mind for the afternoon.

- Decide on the rules for the trip. One rule should be *"No begging for me to give you money."*

- Give a Warning as you get into the car or get to the door of the store. *"Remember, if you beg for money, we leave the store and go home."*

- If the rule is broken, leave immediately. This is inconvenient, but once is all you need to establish that you mean business.

9 Always listen to the entire request. Avoid knee-jerk "no's." A request which starts, "Hey, Mom, look! Model horses. Could I ..." might end with "...buy one," or "put that on my birthday list?"

10 If possible, don't bring your children into those huge toy warehouses. It is too painful for all concerned.

11 If you must shop for a gift for another child, prepare yours: *Today we are shopping for Patricia's present. We won't be buying anything for you today. You may bring along some of your own money, if you think you might want something. Or you can find things to add to your birthday wish list.*

12 If he offers to pay for half the item, you may want to consider this option. It will mean he is willing to commit some of his earnings. For an item you want to encourage, such as a book, you might be willing to fork up half.

If you do decide to "go half-sies" with him, collect the money as soon as you get home, even if it means him giving you an IOU to be deducted from the next allowance. Don't "go half-sies" too frequently, or begging for "half-sies" may be your new problem.

13 If he is continually short of money, have a Family Meeting and introduce the idea of a budget. Help him adjust his spending habits. For example, if he likes books or comics, he can save money by checking them out from the library. You might agree to adjust his allowance or provide him opportunities to earn a little more each week.

SAYING NO and STICKING TO IT:

1 If he begs for money at home or in the car, simply use the Broken Record Technique. Repeat a message such as *"I said 'no' and I mean 'no,'"* until your child gets the picture.

2 If he begs in a store, announce you are going to ignore. *"I will not listen to any more begging about this. End of discussion."* Calmly continue shopping. Get the items you need as quickly as possible, in case you need to make a hasty exit. Ignore any grumblings by paying rapt attention to fine print.

3 If he does not calm down, terminate your errand as rapidly as possible. Announce you are leaving. Swiftly pay for the items you came in for. Proceed calmly but assuredly toward the door, although not so fast as to scare your child. He should be able to see you at all times.

4 If he does not follow you, give him a Warning of a Consequence, *"If you don't leave with me now, you will have a Time-Out."* If he won't come, give him a Time-Out in a quiet corner of the store.

If he refuses to take Time-Out, have a back-up Consequence in mind. *"You either take a five-minute Time-Out now or a fifteen minute Time-Out as soon as we get home."* Another effective back-up Consequence is *"You will lose fifteen minutes of TV time tonight."* I suppose since this is a money-based issue you could have as a Consequence being fined twenty-five or fifty cents.

Whether it is Time-Out, losing TV, being fined, or another Consequence, if your child earns it, you must give it.

5 Make a clear contract with your child before you take him on an errand again. *"The only way you may come shopping with me, is if you bring your own money with you and do not ask me for a loan. If you can agree to that, you may come."*

Too Soon

Somewhere around age nine our kids get a glimpse of the greener pastures of adolescence. Soon they will be chomping at the bit. From nine to twelve, the operative word is "Whoa!"

22
Makeup

THE PROBLEM:

Your 12-year-old (or younger) child wants to wear makeup. She says all her friends do, and that you are just old-fashioned. You want to avoid embarrassment (hers and yours) keep her a child a minute or two longer, and dispel the rumors she's auditioning for Lolita, The Next Generation.

THINKING IT OVER:

Some girls want to grow up fast. As early as age nine their bodies are changing. They anticipate with great excitement their first bra, nylon stockings, heels, and makeup. You may not be ready for the transformation to happen too quickly (or at all!) but your daughter can't wait.

By sixth grade your child will have friends who are wearing makeup to school, with or without parents' permission. She may think it foolish or she may want to do as her friends do. She may or may not understand what makeup can evoke in boys and men, and may or may not accept that your stand against makeup is to protect her until she is old enough to handle reactions to it.

In a couple of years, when she is fourteen or fifteen, you will have to weigh a variety of factors: what her friends do, their pressure upon her, her physical and emotional maturity, your realistic and unrealistic fears for your daughter, your less than stellar reasons for objecting ("I wasn't allowed to wear makeup until my junior year in high school!"), the type of makeup she chooses, and the reactions her made-up looks inspire!

For the parent of a girl twelve or younger, consider saying "yes" to colored lip gloss or nailpolish, but "no" to makeup in public (unless she is involved in a theatrical, dance, or other performance). You may certainly allow makeup for slumber parties or when girlfriends are over.

As with many of these issues of maturation, you and your partner need to see eye-to-eye on the subject or at least be able to fake a united front in order to set the limits you want.

HOW TO KEEP HER FROM WEARING MAKEUP:

1 Make sure you are giving your child lots of attention for her interests, talents, successes, and personal strengths. Her self-esteem should be based upon feeling unconditionally loved by her parents and feeling capable—not on her looks.

2 Enjoy her more age-appropriate attempts to look good or grown up. Maybe she is trying new hairstyles, wearing hats and caps, playing around with matching socks with tops, shoelaces with hair ribbons. This is the age to encourage her creativity and experimentation and to keep your opinions of the results to yourself. If she thinks it's cool, that is the only standard necessary. You may put your foot down if she insists on wearing clothes that are blatantly sophisticated, soiled, or excessively tattered to school or out with you (See Chapter 15, The Wrong Clothes).

3 When she comes to you to ask about makeup or when you discover she is wearing it in public, ask her reasons for wanting to use it at her age. You may find she feels the need to fit in or that she thinks she looks too young or in some other way does not like the way she looks. Use these guidelines to help you listen well:

- Let her have her say. Don't interrupt. Don't try to advise. (Bite your lip if you are a jump-in take-charge sort.)

- Do not make any (not so reassuring) comment like, "But sweetheart, you're so beautiful without makeup." It is not comforting; it feels like you are babying her. And she knows every parent sees their child as beautiful.

- Suppress your smiles when she announces she looks mature enough to carry off wearing makeup. Avoid any impulse you have to resort to sarcasm.

- Be careful not to ridicule her peers; if you can't resist saying something, gently voice your opinion that you think eleven-year-olds look a little young to wear makeup.

- Use the technique of Mirroring (reflecting back her ideas to let her know you can see the situation from her point of view). Tell her you need to talk to her father or mother about her request and that you'll get back to her within twenty-four hours. Such an exchange may go like this:

  Ginny: Okay, Mom, before you say anything, listen to reason. All my friends are wearing lipstick. I can buy it with my own money. And my lips are so chapped and ugly they need it.

  Mom: (uses Mirroring) Let me get this straight. You want to wear lipstick and you're prepared to pay for it yourself and you think it will help your chapped lips. Do I have that right?

  Child. Yeah. So, can I?

  Mom: Wear lipstick.

  Ginny: This is not getting anywhere.

  Mom: (uses Mirroring, then gives Important

Information) Okay. You want a decision from
me. But honey, lipstick actually dries out lips; it
doesn't moisten. Chapstick does that.

Ginny: Mom, you don't know anything. I've used this
moisture-kind at Tracy's and it works great.

Mom: (ignoring the insult and going on) Well, sweetie,
that may be true, but before I make a decision, I
really need to talk this over with your father—

Ginny: Don't tell Dad. He's the one who won't let me
date 'til I'm twenty-five!

Mom: (again, checking it out) You want to wear
lipstick and keep it a secret from you father?

Ginny: It will just be at school and the mall. Why should
he need to know?

Mom: (continuing to Mirror) Ginny, I understand you'd
rather not tell your dad, but I can't make this
decision myself. He's your parent, too.

Ginny: Then let me talk to him.

Mom: That's a good idea. You talk to Dad, and then he
and I will talk. But, Ginny, I don't want you to
get your hopes up. I can't see your dad or I being
comfortable with your wearing lipstick to the
mall or to school until you are older.

4 Talk over your daughter's situation with your partner and set
your in-public and at-home policy about makeup. In a Family
Meeting, share your feelings and decisions with her. Let your
daughter know when and under what circumstances she may wear
lip gloss, blush, or nailpolish. To help her know she won't have to
wait forever, let her know when she will be able to wear lipstick
and other forms of makeup. You might say something like:

Your dad and I feel that you are too young to wear makeup
in public. We have decided you may wear light-colored
nailpolish to school. After school when you're hanging out

at home you can wear whatever you like. We think that
when you are fourteen you can wear colored lip gloss and
by sixteen you may be ready to wear lipstick .

5 If she accepts your decision, thank her.
I know you are disappointed, sweetheart, and I appreciate
your accepting our decision.

SAYING NO and STICKING TO IT:

1 If she does not accept your "no," but shares her feelings in a direct, relatively calm manner (as opposed to screaming and arguing), use Mirroring to let her know you hear her and want to understand. Mirroring helps you make sure you have gotten her message. You don't have to change your mind, but it will help you understand the strong feelings she has.

Example:
Ginny: Dad, everyone in the sixth grade wears makeup!
Dad: So you want to wear makeup to fit in with all
         your friends, is that it?

2 If she does not accept your "no," but resorts to arguing, complaining, or yelling, tell her you're going to ignore:
We have thought about this seriously and our decision is
final. I'm not going to listen to your yelling.

Then turn your attention to something or someone else. If she escalates to a full blown tantrum, simply say, *"The subject is closed."* Find something you need to do in another room and calmly go do it.

3 If—in spite of all your efforts to end the subject—she keeps badgering you, give a Warning of a Consequence:
If you keep screaming at me, you will lose TV (phone,
radio) privileges tonight.

Follow-through with the Consequence if she does not stop the screaming.

4 Always be ready, in spite of heated discussions that you've had, to "praise" your child, when she calmly discusses the matter, shares her feelings in a non-badgering way, presents well-thought out ideas, or accepts your "no" with reasonably good graces. You might say:

I'm glad we could discuss this calmly.

You've really given me a clear picture of the kind of pressure you are under.

I'd be happy for you to have a makeup party here on Friday night for your girlfriends.

I'm glad you accept your mom's and my decision, even if you think we're being too old-fashioned. That shows real maturity.

23
Phone Trouble

THE PROBLEM:

Your child has discovered the phone. She had been indifferent to it all her life and then suddenly the phone seems a permanent extension of her ear. She ties up the phone for hours at a time and is neglecting her schoolwork, family time, and chores. You didn't expect phone trouble until her teens. You want your child, and your phone, back.

THINKING IT OVER:

I didn't think I would need to include a chapter on use of the telephone. My daughter Miranda turned eleven years old and had shown only minimal interest in it, making quick calls to arrange to play with friends. I planned this book for parents of two to twelve-year-olds and I thought to myself, "Miranda at eleven shows no interest, guess the phone issues start at thirteen."

Then at eleven years and five months everything changed. Miranda developed a close friendship with a boy and soon she was on the phone every night. She preferred the phone to TV, playing outside, using the computer, and even her favorite activity, reading.

At first I thought it was kind of cute. Then I found out friends and colleagues were getting a "no answer" signal when they phoned because my daughter was ignoring the beeps that indicated an incoming call. When I complained, she said she "didn't want to be interrupted!"

I also found that instead of being able to use the phone whenever I wanted, which I had been doing all my adult life, I had to wait. I had to listen to Miranda giggle, listen to her friend giggle, tease, and keep up her end of the conversation with, "What? I didn't say that...I didn't...What did you think I said...I did not...What did she say I said...What did you say...You did?" and on and on. I started writing Phone Trouble.

Your preadolescent is rapidly heading toward the most self-absorbed period of life. She is starting to separate from you, to develop her own identity, and to turn to peers. This is not the time she will be extra sensitive to the needs of fellow family members. This is not the time she will be content to sit talking in the living room with her devoted parents if the phone rings and it's for her.

So, limits may be called for. Your goal is to maintain the balance so that every one's phone needs are met. Certainly she can use the phone. The phone is a terrific way for your child to have fun with friends. It's harmless. She's not out after dark, in a car with a young driver, or unsupervised at a mall. No one has ever become pregnant over the telephone, either.

You may or may not yet be ready to share the phone equally with your child (you do pay for the darn thing). You may want to have a double standard or you may be ready for democratic phone usage.

But, either way, setting up some phone-use guidelines is in order.

MAINTAINING SANITY IN A ONE-PHONE HOME:

1 Establish clear rules about phone use that respect every one's needs. Good rules might be:

- Keep your call to ten minutes if someone else needs to use the phone.

- Be courteous to all callers, even little brother's, even big sister's.

- Business, long distance, and emergency calls take priority above all other calls.

- Take messages, if you happen to answer the phone. Write down the information and leave it where you know your family member will find it. (To help facilitate this, put a message pad and pencil at each phone.)

- Decide upon a total time limit for phone usage in an evening, for example, thirty minutes.

- If you have "call waiting," phone users must take all incoming calls (find out who is calling, let your family member know about it) and relinquish the phone in ten minutes.

2 Get the "call-waiting" service so that all family members have an opportunity to get messages or know that someone would like to talk with them. Some parents hate their own calls to be interrupted by incoming "bleeps," but think of how frustrating it is for friends and associates to get a busy signal for hours.

(Don't tell your kids, but you can turn off "call-waiting" when you need to. Before making the call, simply punch in a short code which you can get from your phone company . You will receive no incoming "beeps" during that call. Parties calling in get a busy signal, so they know someone is at home. When you hang up, "call-waiting" is automatically restored.)

3 Avoid the three-way calling service. If you think your child will be on the phone a lot with just one friend, can you imagine how long a call with two other kids could take!

4 Respect your child's conversations. They are private. You may be tempted to eavesdrop a bit, to grill them about who they were talking to, and so forth. This is a good opportunity for you to model respectful behavior (how would you feel if they did these things to you?). It is also a good chance for them to be independent from you, which they need at this point.

5 Try not to get bent out of shape by the content of your child's conversations. They are not interviewing for college, they're doing an intricate developmentally imperative verbal dance that defies adult comprehension. Avoid disappointment. Stay out of earshot.

6 Give your child a When/Then Deal. Tell her when she can use the phone, for example, *"After your homework is done, chores finished and the pets are fed, you may use the phone for one-half hour."*

7 Designate a time period for your child when she can make and receive calls, for example, seven to seven-thirty. You then can tell your friends and colleagues not to bother trying to call you during that half-hour.

8 If you have a cordless phone, insist that the handset be returned to its base or the phone returned to it's proper location, that is, NOT in their room under a pile of clothes. You do not want to have to hunt for the phone when it's ringing.

SAYING NO and STICKING TO IT:

1 I like the rule: "Abuse it, you lose it." Phone abuse might include:

> talking on phone before homework is done
> ignoring incoming calls
> leaving the phone where it can't be found
> using the phone after bedtime
> not informing family members about their messages

using the phone more than an hour a day
ignoring chores because you're on the phone
being rude to callers other than your friends
calling 900 numbers
calling long distance without permission
making crank calls

The logical Consequence for phone abuse is, *"You can't use it for the rest of the day."* If the offense occurs at night, *"You can't use it for twenty-four hours."* If the problem continues, restrict use to the weekends.

If the offense is leaving the phone jacked into the child's room (or under the bed, behind the chair, in the bathroom, beside the TV, at the bottom of a pile of clothes), a good consequence is announcing a new rule, *"No taking away the phone from its permanent location."*

2 Have a Family Meeting to address the phone problems. Use this format:

- State the problem: *"We have a major telephone problem. First of all, the phone rings during dinner and someone disappears for the rest of the meal. I'm not getting messages and Amy says that you younger kids are rude to her friends. Dad tries to call home at 6:30 and can't get through."*

- State how you feel about the problem: *"I am so sick of the phone I want to throw it out."*

- Brainstorm solutions: *"I'm open for suggestions as to how we can respect everyone's needs. Any ideas?"*

- Select a plan to try for a week that everyone can agree on (if your child is sulky or has nothing to add, give a couple of ideas you think will work). For the above family, the plan might include:

1. No calls during mealtimes; use an answering machine, ignore the ringing, or have a family member take messages for every one.

2. Stay off the phone during the regular time Dad tends to call, say from 6:15 until 6:45.

3. Practice with the younger children how to speak courteously to big sister's friends and offer a small reward for excellent phone etiquette.

4. Tie a message pad to each phone; whoever forgets to write or tell a message will be fined fifty cents.

- Have a follow-up Family Meeting to see how the plan is going.

- Decide to keep the plan or adjust it to make it work better.

3 If you are sick and tired of getting the raw end of the phone deal, you can consider giving children their own phone, which they rent from you by doing chores or using their allowance. Phone usage (thank heaven for phone jacks) can be curtailed if they don't pay the rent or if they abuse the phone in any way.

I'm not sure how I feel about a kids' phone, and I haven't been tempted to consider it yet, but I think it may be a necessary act of self-defense, particularly for people who work out of their home or have more than one child who is a heavy phone user.

Don't purchase a phone for a child right on the heals of rotten phone behavior, however. That would be rewarding phone abuse. The next thing you'll know is she'll be telling her friends, "Just drive your parents crazy using it all the time and they'll get you your own phone."First work out the phone etiquette, and then consider having the kids earn their own phone.

If you take this route, keep in mind: "It's a privilege, not a birthright."

24
Pierced Ears
(or Whatever)

THE PROBLEM:

Your child wants to have her (or his) ears—or heaven forbid some other body part—pierced. You want your child to wait.

THINKING IT OVER

In many cultures, baby girls' ears are pierced at birth and in those cultures the value of the tradition outweighs the concern of the momentary hurt for the baby. Those of us who choose not to perform this service to our infant daughters will likely face the issue later on. I do not feel there is a right or wrong age for girls (or boys, for that matter) to have their ears pierced, but I do know piercing raises several issues and that it is a decision which involves the child and her (or his) parents.

When your child pierces her ears is really a matter of your personal values. Piercing is so permanent, so irreversible a decision that some parents would prefer their child was well into her teens, old enough to be certain she would not regret it or mind the momentary pain of the procedure.

One concern for parents is that earrings can signal their daughter's emerging sexuality or provoke question about their son's masculinity. I have seen great dangling earrings on my daughter's sixth grade classmates and a ten-year-old boy at her camp was wearing a tiny loop in his ear. I couldn't help but think, "Now, he's got flexible parents." I imagine many parents are very uncomfortable with both these styles.

You may not even know what bothers you about pierced ears. You may think it is an unnecessary expense (one does need to buy very good earrings to enable healing). You may be concerned she won't take care of her ears adequately and will get an infection. (The child or the parent needs to remember to do the nightly swabbing with alcohol for several weeks and rotate the studs until the wounds heal.)

Having your ears pierced is somewhat painful, and that can be a deterrent. Parents want to avoid the scenario of their child getting one ear pieced and refusing to allow the second one.

Lately, it's not just the matter of two small holes. Girls are having multiple piercings in their earlobes. Some are piercing their noses. Boys may pierce one ear or two. Both men and women are piercing other places I'll not bother mentioning (I saw a teen who had pierced the middle of her tongue!). Hopefully these more unusual perforations won't be the object of your kids' desires until adolescence or later.

One advantage to piercing is that earrings have helped distinguish young short-haired girls from young similarly-coifed boys. A ten-year-old's little ego was spared damage, I am convinced, by her mom's sensitivity to her daughter's needs. She'd gotten an adorable short haircut but was being harassed mercilessly by some schoolmates. A quick trip to the jeweler and Nicki was sporting tiny gold studs. The teasing ceased. (Later, though, the family had to take Nicki to the emergency room for an infection and she's temporarily unable to wear earrings!)

You may find that ear piercing is a bigger deal before hand than after. A single dad friend of mine was adamant against allowing his daughter to be "mutilated" when she was five. After he relented to her pleas a year later he was not quite sure why he had been so against it; it didn't seem like such a big deal. Once you are ready, I think you will be comfortable with your choice, particularly if your child wears age-appropriate earrings, such as studs or tiny loops. If your daughter chooses earrings that make her look like she's playing dress-up, it's too mature a look to sport in public.

KEEPING EARS INTACT:

1 If, after thinking about all the issues and discussing it with your partner, you come to the decision that you are not ready for your child to pierce her ears, try setting a possible date in the future, such as her thirteenth, fifteenth, or even eighteenth birthday. I have always thought that ear piercing is a terrific gift to celebrate an important passage in life, such as graduation from sixth grade, junior high, or upon becoming a teenager.

2 I see no harm in taking full responsibility here for being the Bad Guy. Sometimes we just have to 'fess up to it:

I know you are dying to get your ears pierced and that
Katie has already done hers and she's only ten, but I am
just not comfortable with it. You may pierce your ears
when you are in Junior High.

3 Stand your ground, certainly, but try to be understanding. Listen to her arguments. Empathize with her by using Mirroring.

Kit: But, Mom, you are just so old-fashioned.

Mom: You think I'm just an old fogy?

Kit: Of course. Even babies have pierced ears.

Mom: Yes, some parents do pierce their baby's ears.

Kit: I wish you'd pierced mine when I was a baby.

Mom: Perhaps that would have been best, but we didn't want to do anything that would hurt you. We figured child birth was traumatic enough!

Kit: At least I'd have my ears pierced now.

Mom: That's true, you would have.

Kit: Mom, I'm the only girl in my class who doesn't have her ears pierced.

Mom: Truly, sweetheart? The only one?

Kit: Well, just about.

Mom: No wonder you feel so unhappy.

Kit: So can I do it? Please?

Mom: Honey, your dad and I have talked about this and our decision is for you to wait until you are thirteen. I know you're angry about this, but we have to do what we think is right.

In this example the mother is more interested in hearing her child's hurt and frustration than she is in winning any of the points of discussion. Notice that she does not argue with her daughter, saying, "I'm sure there is are several girls who do not yet have their ears pierced." Kit needs to be heard, not proven wrong.

4 If your daughter is asking for her ears to be pierced for a particular birthday or other occasion, consider another piece of jewelry to memorialize the occasion that would be special for her, such as a locket or a charm bracelet.

SAYING NO and STICKING TO IT:

1 If your child continues to argue, you can continue to empathize with her, but you may also choose to stand your ground. As Kit tries to push her buttons, Mom will ignore her and resist getting pulled into argument.

Kit: Mom, you are being so unfair.

Mom: I imagine that's how it feels, honey.

Kit: Every kid I know, I mean every girl and half the boys even have their ears pierced.

Mom: So I am the only mother who hasn't allowed it?

Kit: Right, the only one who is being a jerk.

Mom: I'm sure that's how it seems.

Kit: I might just pierce them myself, with a needle.

Mom: I couldn't stop you, but I will tell you that when I
        was in college, some kids pierced their ears with
        a needle, ice, and a potato. It was painful, bloody,
        and the holes weren't exactly where they wanted
        them. Some got infected. I hope you wouldn't
        feel you had to go that far.

Kit: That's gross, mom.

Mom: Yes, it was gross.

Kit: But what can I do? You're saying "no" for no
        reason.

Mom: It may not seem like much of a reason, Kit. I just
        feel you are too young to put holes in your head
        and too young to wear earrings.

Kit: You've got holes in your head.

Mom: Yes, but holes or no holes, I have made my
        decision. I'm sorry it makes you unhappy.

Kit is being pretty disagreeable with her mother. You notice mom doesn't get defensive. She allows Kit to vent a bit. Kit's mom wisely ignores her daughter' attempts to strike out at her. This acts as damage-control.

2 If your child starts to scream, cry, make a scene, bang things around, or gets more abusive or colorful in her language, you can calmly leave the room. If you like, say something such as, *"We'll talk more when you are calm,"* or *"That's the end of the conversation."* If you prefer to stay in the room, fine. Grab a magazine or a book. Turn on the TV or pick up the telephone. Do not, however, pay any attention to the sound and fury.

This may not be easy. You may be frightened by her tantrum. Trust me. Your best defense is staying calm and unruffled.

3 If your child threatens to break anything or do any other damage, give a Warning of a Consequence and follow through with giving the Consequence if your child earns it.

Kit, if you break the molding slamming the door, you will pay for it with your allowance.

Remember these elements of an effective Consequence:

It must have meaning for your child;

You must have control over it;

You must be willing to enforce it, and

It should be minimal.

It's nice if the "time fits the crime," and Kit's mom has picked a Consequence that ties in nicely with her slamming about.

You also want a Consequence which you can enforce immediately. The Consequence would be most effective if this were happening on Allowance Day, or if Kit kept her savings in her room rather than in a bank and mom could collect on the spot.

4 If your child takes off with a friend to the mall and shows up sporting metal in her or his ears, you should give your child a Consequence for going against your decision. It may be hard to think of a Consequence. You might choose grounding her from mall-runs with friends for a week or ask for suggestions:

We feel you need a Consequence for going against our decision. We'd like you to think about it and come up with one. If you can't, we will.

Children often come up with quite novel, fair, and appropriate Consequences for their acts. The problem is they often are too hard on themselves.

25
Home Alone with Friends

THE PROBLEM:

Your child begs to be allowed to have friends over or play at a friend's house without parental supervision. You want your child to understand that staying alone with friends is not necessarily safe and that you must say "no."

THINKING IT OVER:

It is clear that some children at the age of eleven, are perfectly capable of being left on their own for short periods of time, if they are physically safe (know what to do in any emergency, have neighbors on "stand-by") and feel emotionally safe (not afraid of being alone). If your child is younger than eleven, it is not advisable that he be left alone. In many places, Children's Services' Workers will investigate if it is reported that a child of ten or younger is left alone for any period of time.

In raising my kids, I find that frequently they want to stay at a friend's house while the parents are out or want friends over while I am out. While you may already allow your child to be home alone for short periods of time, say twenty minutes while you run out to get a carton of milk, I'd advise against leaving your child alone with friends unsupervised.

When children are toddlers we parents are greatly concerned with child-proofing the home environment, the sitter's place, and relatives' and friends' houses. Let's extend this idea to the older child for a moment. What if unsupervised play were to take place at your house? Can you rule out your child and his friends getting into things he should not—matches, cigarettes, alcohol, cleaning chemicals? Some kids like to do kitchen experiments, test out makeup and nailpolish, or engage in other activities which require your supervision. Even if your child would not think of doing these on his own, might he be easily influenced by another? Can you be certain he would assert himself and say, "Hey, we can't do that—my mom and dad will kill me!"

If the issue is playing at the home of another child, how well do you know the parents of this friend? Do you know their habits? Their rules? How well their child follows the rules? Do you know if there is a gun in the house? Whether it is loaded? Whether your child's friend knows where the gun is kept or could find it by accident? What about other adult materials, videos, magazines, and so forth that you would not want your child exposed to?

Even if safety issues are not a concern, an adult around usually provides a sense of warmth and comfort which most children enjoy, but may not cop to wanting. Of course, with older kids that comfort is established even if the adults keep themselves well out of sight (which is what they prefer).

Here then, is my permission for you to be a little fussy, a little cautious, and a little over-protective when it comes to leaving kids unattended. Your own child may be quite mature and trustworthy, but you can't plan for all potential danger. You don't have to be invasive and overbearing, but you do need to make sure your children are safe.

HOME ALONE—NOT!!!!:

1 As our children grow they require increased independence, opportunities to explore, and opportunities to develop responsibility. If it is safe in the neighborhood, the four-year-old benefits from being able to walk to a neighbor's (on the same side of the street in busy areas). A seven or eight-year-old feels a wonderful freedom in walking a block or two to visit. If the community is safe, walking to school at ten might be ideal.

But you must always differentiate between experiences which allow freedom and experiences which expose a child to danger. If, as he grows, you share your reasons for allowing certain privileges, denying others, all the while attempting to be fair and realistic, your child will know you have his best interest at heart. He may not be happy with your restrictions, however.

2 Use the experiences of parents you respect to support your choices, particularly if you tend to be too restrictive or too permissive. Find out how their children handle privileges; ask what has worked in their home. Experiences of others may give you the best insight into establishing family rules.

3 Your child's temperament may be a more accurate measurement than his age in determining safety guidelines. The child who is cautious by nature may handle freedom in a more thoughtful way than the impulsive child.

4 Establish your "Home Alone" rule in a family talk when being home alone is not an immediate issue. For your child to take you seriously, you may need to take advantage of a grim TV or newspaper report of a domestic disaster, such as a fire or an accidental shooting, which has occurred when kids were left unattended.

Make sure your child understands the rule clearly, *"If Andrew's parents aren't home, you are not allowed to play there. Come home."* Or the rule might be, *"You may only play outside if his parents aren't at home,"* or *"You need to call me from Andrew's house if his parents need to leave."*

5 Don't break the home alone rule yourself, no matter how tempted you might be. You may have a house full of responsible eight and nine-year-olds and discover you're out of milk. How dangerous could it be, you might think, to run to the corner convenience store? The danger to the kids may be minimal, but your child will remember your breaking the rule. "But Dad! You left us alone when you ran out of milk, remember? Nothing happened, right?" It's hard to argue with his logic.

6 Begin to exert extra caution when your child can call a friend and invite himself over to his house, then run out the door hollering over his shoulder, "I'll be at David's—." Stop your little guy in his tracks and find out exactly what his plans are. Who's house is he heading for, how long will he be there, who will be there, who will not be there, and so forth. If your child's expectation is that he wants to stay with a friend with parents gone, tell him why it is unsafe and that the answer is "no."

It won't hurt to have your child call when he arrives at his friends, let you talk to a parent, and present your expectations: that if the parents need to leave they are to send your child home.

7 It is hard to cover all bases as your child becomes more independent and you have less control. My son Kyle now knows to say to me, "I'm going up to Jack's house. If his mom's not there, I'll come back. Or I might just go to David's. I'll call you." And he does. But it took a lot of trial and error to establish those patterns.

SAYING NO and STICKING TO IT:

1 When your child asks to play alone with a friend, remind him of the rule and let him know his options. You can say, *"Invite Enrique over now and then you two can go to back to his house later, when his mom or dad gets back."*

2 If he keeps nagging you to stay home alone with a friend or be allowed to go a friend's house when parents aren't there, stand your ground by using the Broken Record Technique. Select a short phrase like, *"The answer is no,"* or *"The subject is closed,"* and repeat it in response to all arguments.

Tim: Why can't I play at Enrique's without his mom home?

Mom: Tim, I've explained it to you several times. The subject is now closed.

Tim: You just don't trust kids.

Mom: The subject is closed.

Tim: Mom, you're not fair.

Mom: The subject is closed.

Tim: Why do you treat me like a baby?

Mom: The subject is closed.

3   Since this is a safety issue and there is little new information which will change your mind, simply ignore arguments, fusses, and tantrums, once you have clearly laid out the reasons for your rule.

4   If the protests become too long, too loud or for any reason intolerable, use a Warning of a Consequence. Make eye contact with your child, give your Warning calmly but firmly, and be ready to follow through.

If you kick the table one more time, you will not be able to have Enrique come over for a half-hour.

5   Of course, if he does kick the furniture, you must follow through with the Consequence. *"Okay, Tim, no friends over until 10:30."* If another tantrum ensues, *"Stop the screaming or I will make it 11:00."* That should do it. (Give him a half-minute or so grace period to get himself under control.).

Remember, when your child finally becomes his old self again, be ready to move on and respond to his positives with your positives.

6 If your child sneaks out to a friend's house when the parents aren't home, he should be given a Consequence. For example, you might Ground him from seeing that particular friend for the rest of the day or Ground him from playing away from home for the next day.

26
Dating

THE PROBLEM:

Your child wants to date (translation: go out at night with someone of the opposite sex without adult supervision). You can't believe it and you'd rather not deal with it at all.

THINKING IT OVER:

If this whole subject strikes you as absurd, don't be too hasty. As a social worker I have met teenage mothers as young as eleven and twelve, teenage fathers not much older. Kids are moving at a faster pace these days. And although some actually are maturing physically earlier than their parents and grandparents, physical maturation does not bring emotional maturation. Ten, eleven, and twelve-year-olds are not sixteen, seventeen, and eighteen-year-olds. They still need their parents to reduce the pressure to grow up with a clear message such as, "Dating at twelve is out of the question. You may date when you are sixteen."

Forgive me, if I make the assumption that for the ten, eleven, and twelve-year-old set, the dating issue mostly applies to girls. Girls mature faster, get mistaken for fourteen, fifteen, and sixteen-year-olds by older boys, and are more readily tempted to date. Certainly if your boy is pressuring you to allow him to date girls his age, or older girls for that matter, use the guidelines presented here to set appropriate limits.

Not every boy/girl situation is an occasion for panic, however. Chaperoned events such as dances, picnics, film festivals, sports events, or potlucks, sponsored by your school, community, town, church, temple, social or political group, are excellent "first date" possibilities which might be appropriate for the sixth or seventh grader. Outings with the family of a friend of the opposite sex— going bowling, seeing a film, or going skating or to play miniature golf—can give your child the feelings of independence from you and the excitement of being with someone she likes a lot. These can be valuable experiences which help your child work out the difficult and complicated social pathway to adult relationships.

Don't assume that a relationship with someone of the opposite sex will be romantic or sexual. Girls and boys below the age of thirteen are capable of, in fact prefer, friendships which have no sexual content whatsoever. Such friendships can be important in helping your child understand the workings of the opposite sex (not always an easy feat!). Your child's temperament, values, interests, and levels of self-awareness, self-esteem, and responsibility will help determine the amount of supervision she requires.

As your child approaches adolescence, your number one challenge is to keep communication open. She is not going to want you "in her face," so you need to stay back a bit. At the same time you want to provide an atmosphere in which it will be easy for her to talk to you. The more you are talking, the more you will be able to pick up the danger signs of potentially unsafe relationships.

You need to decide on the messages you want to give your kids and the guidelines you expect them to follow. In order to do this parents must be communicating with each other. This may not be too easy. Dad: Are you ready to face that your little girl is starting to mature, is wearing a bra in the fifth grade, may start getting phone calls from boys, may get her period any day? And you

Mom: Soon you will have a pre-teen guy in your house. How will you help him deal with his physical and emotional changes? Voice cracking, body perspiring, and more? How do you want him treating young women? The way you were treated by young men? I know they aren't teenagers yet, but don't blink, it comes all too quickly.

So put your heads together and clarify your values. When do you want your child to date? What is your stand on unsupervised parties? How do you want your child to treat others or be treated? What are the values you would like to communicate to her or him, and the conditions under which you want your child to become sexually active.

Start talking to your kids. Without your input, they'll do it their own way or their friends' way. With your input they may hold on to some of your values.

HOW TO POSTPONE INTEREST IN DATING:

1 Don't ask your toddlers and small children if they have a boyfriend or girlfriend. This might lead them to think they need one.

2 Set limits on television and movies. You probably don't want Hollywood to be influencing your child more than you are.

3 Expose your child to a variety of activities. As they round the age of nine and ten girls start being interested in rock music, makeup, jewelry, more sophisticated clothes, and anything connected with teenage life. Make sure there is equal time allowed for other diversions: music, art, theatre, skating, bicycling, softball, tennis, books, cooking, science, and more. Introduce these if she is not already aware of them.

4 Teach them respect for others' feelings and bodies. Correct disrespectful attitudes or behaviors. Your values will come to displace the ones they are picking up from school or the park. The summer my son Kyle was seven he attended a day camp. He was practicing a skit that several boys had put together. Kyle's dad listened and then said, *"You know, Kyle, you guys might not have meant it that way, but the script makes fun of girls' bodies and could really hurt their feelings or make them angry."* A couple of days later Kyle was still rehearsing, but the words were different. "We decided the other skit was sexist, so we're doing a new one," he explained. He had taken his dad's words to heart, told his buddies at camp, and they had agreed to a change. Correcting disrespectful attitudes can help your child and others.

5 Make your values clear to your child. It's okay to be straightforward. For example, in the arena of boyfriends, you might say, *"Although I cannot stop you from liking someone best, I would prefer that you did not have a steady boyfriend until you are in high school or older."* I'd stop short of frequent nagging or lecturing.

6 Provide parties with adult supervision. Give kids free choice on food, music, the friends to be invited (kids her own age only), and some flexibility on the hours. Don't hover, but be there. Give clear directions to your child. Have her tell you if these occur: kids using bedrooms, turning lights off, pairing up and disappearing, using drugs or any adult substances, such as cigarettes, alcohol or x-rated videos.

7 Give her new privileges each year, so that she doesn't go from eight-year-old limits to sixteen-year-old limits without increasing opportunities to learn to handle responsibility. A later bedtime, scheduling her homework time herself, studying alone at the library, staying for short periods of time without a sitter, eventually (when she is comfortable) staying alone for an evening, and using public transportation are good steps towards independence.

8 Keep talking to your child. Find a semi-regular time you and she can touch base. Bedtime is a great time for a quiet, relaxed talk. Don't pry, just be available. If you have a hard time talking to your daughter or son, maybe your spouse would be more comfortable with it. I don't think it matters who does the talking (actually, it's the listening that's important), just that it take place.

9 Get to know your child's friends. You may find it harder as she gets older and meets kids beyond the block or outside your circle of friends. When your child is little you can visit her classroom on occasion, but by fifth or sixth grade parents are not usually as welcome. If you drive your child to school take a moment at drop-off or pick-up time to exchange brief hello's with the kids she's hanging out with. Have her invite one or two or even a small group over for a Friday night pizza party. Meet her friends' parents at your school's fundraising events and open houses. These don't have to become fast friendships, just acquaintances. Your son or daughter is hanging out at their houses and you will want to know who they are.

10 Provide health and sex education at an early age. There are great books about the body and all its parts and workings. Be candid and open in answering questions. Take your lead from them—you don't want to embarrass your kids—but feel free to have talks about maturing, sexuality, dating, and what adolescence will be like. Lynda Maderas has a marvelous series of books, including *The What's Happening to My Body Book for Girls* (and a similar one for boys). Make use of this wonderful time in your life when your child wants to tell you how she feels.

11 Trust your youngster unless you have very good reason not to. Don't assume—without major evidence—that your child is breaking your rules or is intent on a life of sex, drugs and rock 'n roll. Don't be too quick to threaten convent or military school at the first phone call from someone of the opposite sex. You may find yourself driving your child into less than terrific behaviors.

I have met several young teens whose parents were so suspicious and accusatory of their children's behaviors that the kids stopped trusting their parents with information about their lives. The children, innocent to begin with, began to experiment with just those behaviors their parents were suspicious of. The kids became sneaky and evasive, developing the attitude, "Well, I'm being accused of it, I might as well do it." Interestingly enough, several of those parents had been out of control teenagers themselves and expected no better of their kids. I cannot adequately share with you the sense of hopelessness these young kids feel when their parents no longer believe they are "good kids."

One twelve-year-old child recently said to me, "I open up to my mom and she uses it against me. If we're riding in the car I don't even make eye contact with guys we pass, 'cause she says, 'You better not even think about getting together with someone like that!' I can't even look at guys!"

Provide clear and reasonable expectations and then trust your child and her good judgment. If your child begins to engage in behaviors which concern you, seek the guidance of a family counselor who specializes in children and adolescents who will help you put the behaviors in context of her age and development, and help you walk the fine line between over- and under-reacting.

SAYING NO and STICKING TO IT:

1 Make sure you understand what your child means by her question, "Can I go out on a date?" Does she possibly mean a chaperoned event? Maybe it wouldn't even occur to her to go to a drive-in with a sixteen-year-old at this age. Maybe she is thinking about a small group going to an arcade, being dropped off at the mall for a movie, or meeting a friend at the ice-cream shop. She might want to go to an amusement park with her friend's big sister and boyfriend or even (yes!) study with a buddy at the library. Get more information on what she has in mind, before you panic.

2 If a friend has initiated the invitation, find out how your child feels about it. Many kids would be uncomfortable with a very adult offer and extremely relieved to hear you say, "Not on your life." Before you jump in with your two cents' worth say, *"I'm wondering how you feel about this. When I was your age I would have felt a bit uncomfortable."* That might help your child express her true feelings about the invitation.

3 When your child gets any invitation, call the other kid's parents. Make sure an adult will be present and that the situation is one which meets your safety standards. If your child balks, say simply, *"Sweetie, I'm not doing this to embarrass you, but because it's my job to keep you safe."* If she starts to tantrum, calmly say, *"In order for you to go with Jack's family, I need to talk with his parents."* If she refuses to let you call, you may refuse to let her go.

4 Think positively. Decide what you can say "yes" to. There may be several choices for your child. Save your "no" for her asking, "May I go out with a boy alone on a date?"

5 Don't lecture; kids hate being lectured to. Make it clear once that this is the only decision you can make as a responsible parent, then spare her the lecture.

6 If, after you have put your foot down, she wants to talk about it in a calm manner, fine. Listen to her, hear her arguments, and try to understand her point of view. Stick to your decision unless you discover her definition of dating involves doubling with her parents. Do let her know what you will allow, *"Although you may not go to the mall with him, you may have Alex over to our house for pizza and a video."*

7 If you have to say no, be prepared to ignore tantrums, screaming, insults, name-calling, sighs, rolling eyes, swearing and other reactions designed to get your goat. Make eye contact, say calmly *"The subject is closed,"* turn away, and grab a juicy novel. Keep your eyes on the page even if the words blur. If she persists, resort to the Broken Record Technique. Repeat *"The subject is closed,"* until she gets bored or disgusted and stamps off to her room.

8 If she should break your rule, and sneak out on an unsupervised date, give an appropriate Consequence, such as losing phone privileges for twenty-four hours or being Grounded for the upcoming weekend evenings. Afterwards, proceed with caution, but not paranoia. Hope that your child has learned a lesson and give her opportunity to re-earn your trust.

Glossary

Throughout the book, examples are given of the following tools and terms. I thought you would want a concise reference to them. So look on the following pages to learn more about:

Announcement
Better Behavior Chart
Brainstorming
Broken Record Technique
"Catch Them Being Good"
Child Development/Developmental Age
Choice Time
Choices
Command
Consequence
Diaries, Journals, and Feeling "Books"
Family Meeting
Grounding
Ignoring
Invitation Back to the Family
Mirroring (Active or Empathic Listening)
Praise and Positive Attention
Reminder
Temperament
Time-Out
Treasure Box
Trial Run
Warning
"What's Your Plan?"
When/Then Deal

Announcement

An Announcement lets your child know she must soon stop what she is doing and do something else. Give a five, ten, or at most fifteen minute Announcement before you need her to stop playing. When the time has lapsed, say, *"The time is up now. We have to go."* Praise her when she complies.

If your kids don't tell tell time yet, carry a timer (*"When the timer rings it will be time for lunch."*), or give them a measurement they can understand (*"When your turn is over, we'll need to put away the game,"* or *"Four more times down the slide, and then we'll go."*).

Better Behavior Chart

A BBC is a posted record which reminds your child of his daily tasks in a fun, non-nagging way, while it reminds you to praise him as he successfully completes the daily tasks. Here is how to set up a BBC for homework:

1. Choose five or six daily goals for your child. Be sure that three of the goals are easy tasks for him. Include the time you want the task finished, the number of reminders you will give, and any help he needs.

2. Arrange the goals on a chart in chronological order. A homework-oriented chart might have these behaviors:
    Brings home assignment book with teacher's signature.
    Brings home all necessary materials to do homework.
    Finishes homework at daycare (by 5:30) and puts it in backpack.
    Shows homework to Mom or Dad and makes corrections by 7:30.
    Puts homework in backpack before bed.

3. For ten school days, without your child's knowledge, record his successes at completing the tasks (Private Records). If your child is earning at least one-third of the possible successes, your chart is challenging, but not too challenging, and you can introduce him to it.

    If he does not do about one-third of the tasks successfully, then the chart is too difficult. Substitute a very easy task to boost his success-rate. Studies have shown that if you praise behaviors which have a high compliance rate (children do easily and readily) they actually increase their compliance for other behaviors.

4. Go Public. Sit down with your child and introduce the chart. Say:
    This is a plan to help you do your homework. Each time you do one of the tasks you'll earn a sticker. We can put up the chart on the fridge, in your room, wherever you like. Every night I'll give you a

*small reward for every sticker you earned that day. I was thinking
of a dime, a jelly bean, a baseball or comic card.*

5. For an older child, set a goal to work toward based on the number of
    successes you counted during Private Records. If he completed ten
    behaviors the first week and eleven behaviors the second, you can be
    pretty certain he will succeed at ten of the tasks. You can offer him this
    deal:
    *If you earn at least ten stickers, on Saturday when we go grocery
    shopping I'll give you fifteen cents for every sticker. Ten stickers
    will earn you a dollar fifty for video games.*

6. As he meets his goal and surpasses it, up the ante a bit the next week; he
    might have a target of eleven or twelve.

7. If a child fails an item, ignore it. If he's upset, say simply, *"Tomorrow
    you'll have another chance. But look, you got three today, that's great!"*

8. Use a BBC for three to four weeks until the new habits have replaced
    the old ones. Use as needed to inspire more cooperation.

Brainstorming

Brainstorming is a terrific way for you and your kids to come to a decision
about a family conflict. First you identify the problem. Then everyone
involved rapidly throws out ideas on how to solve it. One person jots them
down. No one may comment on or censor them. Continue until you run out
of solutions.

Go through the list of ideas and cross out the ones anyone has trouble
with and circle the ideas that everyone would be willing to try.

Pick the most popular and agree to try it out for three to five days.

Set a meeting to assess whether it worked.

If it did not work, try another from the list.

Broken Record Technique

The Broken Record Technique is the simple repeating of a Command when
your child argues with you. Stay calm and don't change your message. (If
the child gives *you* the BRT, use a Warning of a Consequence instead.)

Example:

Xavier: Why can't I hang out at the mall with Billy?

Dad: Xavier, I already told you "no" several times and I have
         told you why. The subject is closed.

Xavier: That's not fair! Why can't we even talk about it?

Dad: The subject is closed.

Xavier: Billy's dad said it was all right with him. He trusts us.
Dad: The subject is closed.
Xavier: What could go wrong? What could happen?
Dad: The subject is closed.
Xavier: Great! Thanks a lot. (Stomps off)

"Catch Them Being Good"

"Catch them Being Good" is a phrase used by UCLA's Parent Training Program. The idea is that in any situation, parents should try to acknowledge the child's good behavior, while ignoring misbehavior (unless, of course, it is hurtful or harmful). This is because any attention a parent gives is, in fact, a reward which will increase the behavior.

Suppose you have been nagging your child to clean his room all afternoon. Finally he stomps off toward his room, mumbling under his breath. You dislike the stomping and the mumbling, yet he is headed toward his room. He might be going to clean it. When we recognize this "small step in the right direction" and acknowledge it with a simple "Thank you," we "catch him being good." We have seen a lot of negative, but have found one positive, and have praised the child's effort.

The parent in this case might check on his child a few minutes later and if there has been any small effort to begin straightening his room, the parent can offer encouragement or help.

Child Development/Developmental Age

All children go through stages of intellectual, social, physical and emotional development. Each child develops at his own rate and may be early in one area, a little behind in another, and right on target in another. There are certain stages we can expect our child to go through and we recognize the signs of these stages. The two-year-old seeks independence, the four-year-old wants control, and so forth. It is helpful to read about child development. Many a parent has picked up a classic, read that eight-year-olds are sensitive to criticism, and been relieved beyond belief that his child's recent moodiness is normal, in fact, right on target. You still need to deal with the difficulties of the stage, but you don't have to feel so alone.

Read about the age your child is now, last year and next year. That way you can get a real feel for what to expect and how your child is maturing compared to his age mates.

If your child has a developmental disability, you can determine his developmental age by reading about different ages and stages. If you find that your eight-year-old is socially behaving at about a five-year-old level, for example, you then have a jumping off point for figuring out what is appropriate to expect of her. You might find five-year-old playmates which would be appropriate for her.

Choice Time

Choice Time is a daily period of twenty or so minutes when the child gets to choose any play activity she'd like. Parents can be part of Choice Time if they like, with your child choosing the activity, or Choice Time can be solitary play. You can set some limitations on it (no paints just before bedtime, for example). A parent who had few available Consequences came up with Choice Time so that she'd have a privilege to take away in increments of five minutes.

Turn off the TV, or you will lose five minutes of Choice Time.

Finish your homework by 7:30, and you'll have your full twenty-five minutes of Choice Time tonight.

Choices

A Choice is the offer of two options. Underlying the offer is the understanding that your child must choose one or the other. Choices are often easier to accept than a direct command. Praise your child when she makes her choice, however reluctantly.

Command: *"Go put on your pajamas."*

Choice: *"Do you want to wear your striped pj's or your red ones?"*

Command

A Command is a simple statement to start or stop a behavior. To give an effective Command you should establish eye contact with your child, name the behavior you want started or stopped, and use a neutral, firm tone. Give a reminder or two if necessary. And never lecture.

Don't ask a question: "Can you pick up your room now?"

Give a firm command: *"It's time to pick up your room."*

Consequence

A Consequence is a loss of a privilege:

- Which has meaning for the child,
- Over which you have control,
- Which you are willing to take away,
- Is minimal in duration.

Workable Consequences:
>   earlier bedtime by 5-15 minutes
>   no TV for evening or loss of first ten minutes of favorite program
>   no use of phone
>   loss of Choice Time
>   coming in from play for two to ten minutes
>   loss of use of toy for two to ten minutes
>   one to ten minute Time-Out

Try always to give a Warning before giving a Consequence (See Warning).

Diaries, Journals, and Feeling "Books"

Two wonderful techniques for helping children with hurts that can't be fixed:

- Keep a journal. Give a diary or blank book to your older child and suggest that he write in it about his feelings. With a child who can't write or can't write as fast as his thoughts come, you be "the pencil." Tell your child, *"I am the pencil. You tell the words to me and I'll write them down. Pencils don't talk so I won't either. I won't get mad or laugh."* Your child will come to treasure his diary, finding it a welcome ear for troubles. You'll see him re-reading it or even sharing it with friends.

- Make a "book," when your child has a hurt, problem, or loss. For toddlers, make a picture book of a couple of pages. Ask the child to tell the story. Write down the words under the pictures. Staple the pages together. Make other books as your child has emotional or physical hurts, anticipates changes in his life or needs to soothe the greater traumas of separation, divorce or death of a loved one (or pet). Your child will keep these books and you'll find him pouring over them time after time.

Family Meeting

(Also see Brainstorming)

When parents want their children to participate in the solving of a problem, call a Family Meeting. The steps in a Family Meeting are:

1. Define the problem. Make sure you identify the issues behind the problem, what makes the problem a problem. Example:
    Problem: Your nine-year-old child has been sneaking off the playground after-school and going to a convenience store with other kids.

Issues for parents: the sneaking, lack of safety at the convenience store, breaking school rules, no crosswalks, no supervision.
Issues for child: all his friends do it, he's hungry after school.

2. Brainstorm solutions to the problem. Make sure every one's issues have been addressed. For this problem:
    *   Parents might send snack for kid and his two best buddies.
    *   Convenience store might be approached to clear out the panhandlers and drunks hanging outside.
    *   Child should be allowed to go with sixth grader.
    *   Parents might pressure community to provide crosswalk.
    *   Parents might call other kids' parents and talk with them.
    *   Parents might call school and insist on better supervision.

3. Select solution or solutions which everyone can agree on.

4. Try out solutions and set a date for a follow-up meeting in three to five days to assess how things are going.

    This family might have concluded that there will be a consequence for leaving the playground without permission, that parents will pack a snack big enough to share with his friends, that they will call the school and insist on better supervision, and that they will arrange with a sixth grader to accompany the kids every other Friday for an ice-cream at a nearby drugstore which has a safer atmosphere.

5. Have the follow-up meeting. If the plan is working, continue it. If not pick another solution from your "brainstorm" to try out for a time.

Grounding

Grounding is a Consequence for misbehavior, in which parents require a child to stay in the house for a determined period of time. It may include restriction on phone use or other in-home privileges. Grounding usually becomes an option when kids are older and can play outside with neighbor kids, go to friends' houses, ride their bikes in the neighborhood.

To be an effective Consequence it has to meet certain criteria:
*   Does grounding have *meaning* for the child?
    Yes, if your child likes to go outside and has friends she wants to get together with. Maybe not, if your child's greatest pleasure is to stay home and read or shoot hoops in the back yard.
*   Do you have *control* over it? Will your child stay grounded?

Yes, if your child will stay in when you tell her to. No, if your child will climb out a window or sneak out the back door.

- Are you *willing* to ground your child?
  Yes, if it's not a struggle. Perhaps not, if your child will make life miserable while she's grounded.

- Is grounding *minimal* in duration?
  Yes, if you ground for the afternoon or twenty-four hours, possibly the weekend for a very serious offense. No, if you are grounding for a week or more.

Ignoring

Ignoring is a very effective technique to reduce behaviors you dislike. When you ignore you give your child two messages, "This is a behavior I dislike," and, "You'll get no payoff or attention from me as long as you continue." To ignore effectively:

Turn away from your child.
Break eye contact.
Keep a neutral, detached expression (show no anger).
Say nothing.
Show no emotion.
Ignore immediately—as soon as he starts the behavior.
Praise as soon as your child stops the behavior or starts one you like.

You can tell your child you are going to ignore with an announcement:

I am not going to talk to you until you can use a quiet voice.
The subject is closed.
When you can ask nicely, I will discuss it.
As long as you use that language, my ears aren't working.

Invitation Back to the Family

A neutral statement that lets your child know you are no longer angry, that you are willing to have him join the family. It's helpful to use an Invitation Back to the Family after you have given your child a Consequence. The child may be pouting, angry at you, angry at himself, unable to clear the air. Ask him a question: "Thought we'd have hamburgers for supper, Kenny, what do you think?" Or "After supper I want to rent a video. Any ideas on something we could all watch together?"

Your child may not take the bait, may want to sulk further, may go so far as to say, "I hate videos (or hamburgers)." If he does, just ignore the remark.

Don't beg. Calmly walk away and try later. At least he'll know you have let go of your anger and after awhile he will be able to as well.

Mirroring (Active or Empathic Listening)

Mirroring is a way of listening and giving feedback which lets your child know you know how he feels. You try to understand the situation from his point of view and check it out with him (to make sure you've got it right).

We parents are often great at giving reasons and at giving advice, but reasoning does not sooth hurt feelings:
Kid: Why can't I have a kitty?
Dad: We have no room for a kitten.
Kid: She can live in my room.
Dad: But honey, you're not old enough to take care of a kitten.
Kid: Yes I will! I promise I'll take care of it!

Nor does giving advice help a child:
Kid: I want a kitty.
Dad: How about if you play with the kitty next door?
Kid: I want *my* kitty, daddy.
Dad: How about if we go to the zoo this weekend and see big tiger kitties?
Kid: I want little kitties.

The Mirroring response allows a child to feel her dad accepts her feelings, even if it doesn't fix the situation:
Kid: I want a kitty sooooo bad.
Dad: Sounds like you really want a kitty.
Dad: I know how much you really want a kitty, sweetheart, but we can't.
Kid: (cries)
Dad: You're very disappointed, aren't you.
Kid: (cries more)
Dad: You wish I could fix it, don't you?
Kid: (nods)
Dad: I'm sorry you feel so sad.

NOTE that in this last example, the father is mirroring his child's feelings as closely as he can. When you mirror feelings, you give permission for her to express even more—so tears or anger may come before the child feels any relief.

Praise and Positive Attention

By using Positive Attention or Praising, you can increase children's behaviors. The elements of Positive Attention are:

- Go to your child or have your child come to you.
- Get on a level with your child, lean toward her.
- Make eye contact.
- Praise the action or behavior, not the child. Name the behavior.
- Smile if you feel like it.
- Your tone should express the good feeling you have about the behavior you're praising.
- Praise immediately.
- Avoid sarcasm or an "I told you so" response

Examples of praise:

> *Great job starting your homework without a reminder!*
> *Thanks for finding your shoes so quickly.*
> *I appreciate your being so polite at Nana's house.*

Reminder

You may need to give a Reminder to your child even after you have given a clear Command. That's okay. Think of it as the extra little help all children need. Simply repeat the Command in a calm, firm voice. Don't get angry, don't turn up the heat. You'll be surprised that giving one or two Reminders results in pretty quick compliance. If you need more than two, that's nagging; feel free to use a Warning of a Consequence.

Temperament

The way one reacts to his or her environment. Some are calm, some are more high-strung, for example. Temperament is innate and many parents will claim, "He was the most good-natured baby, right from birth." Temperament may not change, but behavior can.

Time-Out

Time-Out is an all-purpose, portable Consequence. It comes from the phrase "time out from reinforcement," meaning a time when the child will get no response for his actions. It is best to use Time-Out as a Consequence for one hurtful or destructive behavior at a time; you do not want to be using it all day long every day or it may lose its impact.

Let's see if it meets the criteria of an effective Consequence:

- Does Time-Out have *meaning* for your child?
  Yes, most kids through the age of twelve do not like Time-Out. Avoid giving Time-Out in the bedroom, however, or it may turn into fun.

- Do you have *control* over it?
  Yes, if your child will stay in the Time-Out chair when you tell him to. No, if your child will out-and-out refuse to stay put.

- Are you *willing* to give your child Time-Out?
  Yes, it is a firm, non-physical, not overly punitive consequence.

- Is Time-Out *minimal*?
  Yes, if you use the guideline one minute per year of child's age or less.

To use a Time-Out effectively, follow these guidelines:

1. Pick a place for Time-Out. A near-by chair turned toward the wall works great.

2. Pick a length of time for Time-Out. One minute per year of child's age or less is sufficient.

3. When a destructive or hurtful behavior starts, give a Warning of Time-Out. Say, *"The rule is no hitting. If you hit, you will have Time-Out. We're going to practice right now. Here is a chair. If you hit, I will say, 'Alex, go to the Time-Out chair.' When Time-Out is over we will tell you."*

4. If she continues the behavior, give her Time-Out.

5. If she resists with arguing but sits in the chair, ignore the arguing. If she half-sits, half-lies on the chair or slides on to the floor, simply ignore. She's not having that much fun.

6. If she refuses to go into Time-Out, give her the Choice of Time-Out or another Consequence. "You either take a five minute Time-Out now, or lose fifteen minutes of your TV show tonight."

7. When Time-Out is over do not lecture, soothe, explain, or cuddle, as this might actually increase the negative behavior. Some children will do a bad behavior and tolerate the Time-Out, in an attempt to get the expected cuddling. Just say "Your Time-Out is over." In a few minutes you may give her an Invitation Back to the Family.

Treasure Box

A Treasure Box is a collection of goodies and doodads which can be wrapped or unwrapped. Good Treasure Box items are: inexpensive, non-perishable leftovers from any holiday, stickers, small boxes of crayons, marbles, or simply pieces of paper rolled up and tied with yarn on which you write activities (playing music tapes, dancing with mom for 15 minutes, painting project, being read to, reading to mom or dad, sending a postcard to grandparent, going for a walk with the dog, visit to a library, twenty minute bike-riding lesson, making a collage, renting a videotaped movie, baking cookies, having a tea party, inviting a friend to spend an overnight).

In return for terrific behavior, your child gets to choose from the box. You must be willing to do your part immediately when your child has earned a right to pick a treasure.

Trial Run

A "Trial Run" is just what it says, a trial. You get to practice your limit setting skills while your children get to practice reasonable behavior. You know it's a trial, they don't.

One reason parents are less than effective in public is that they lack confidence. They wonder what others are thinking; they're certain it can't be good. They may not even try to set limits on their kid for fear of failure. The Trial Run gives you confidence, because you know exactly what you will do at every turn.

Let's apply the trial run to the problem of Grocery Store Begging:

1. Plan a shopping trip. Keep your list short and choose things you could live without.

2. Remind your child of the rule "No begging while we shop." Warn him that if he breaks the rule you will take him home immediately.

3. Enter the store and praise any terrific behaviors you see (or even any okay ones!)

4. If he breaks a rule, calmly announce you are leaving. Park the cart with the manager and leave the store. Ignore protests, graciously accept apologies, and walk directly to the car.

6. Deposit your child with your partner, a sitter, or neighbor and return to the market.

The Trial Run should establish your credibility. Your Rules and Warnings will have more power and you will feel more confident in public.

Warning

(Please read Consequence too)

A Warning is the promise to your child of the consequence you will give unless your child starts or stops a certain behavior. Use a Warning when your child starts a behavior that is hurtful or harmful to others. Also use a Warning when your child ignores a Command and you need to go to another level of limit setting.

Unless the situation is dangerous, always try to give a Warning before giving a Consequence. (The exception to this is hitting sibling; you can use a "standing warning" for that.) The Warning gives your child the opportunity to take responsibility for his own actions. He can continue with the behavior or stop the behavior and get praise.

"What's Your Plan?"

"What's Your Plan?" is a simple question that puts responsibility on your child for solving the problem at hand. "What's Your Plan?" implies, "There needs to be a plan and if you don't come up with one, I will." If you have a child who responds cooperatively to "What's your plan?" then you will not have to use as many direct Commands.

Here is an example of using "What's Your Plan?" to a child who is watching TV on Saturday morning at 9:30 am:

Dad: Leslie, your softball game starts at noon and you have chores to do this morning. What's your plan for getting those done?

Leslie: After I finish my program, Dad.

Dad: That sounds fine. May I give you a reminder at 10?

Leslie: Okay.

Dad: Great.

If this sounds like a little on the miraculous side, try it. With some children, it works well.

When/Then Deal

A When/Then Deal is the agreement to give a privilege in exchange for a behavior or task. It's a low conflict way of getting children to cooperate, because they will earn a privilege in return. You don't have to nag, because it's up to the child to do the task. The only consequence of not doing the task is that he forfeits the privilege.

The When/Then Deal (also the If/Then Deal) is a good tool to use before you have to resort to warnings. Examples:

When you've done your homework, then you may ride your bike.

When you can get up at 6:30 without a fuss, then you may have a later bedtime.

When you can speak to me in a reasonable voice, then I will listen.

If you will play quietly so that I can work for a while, then I'll read you a story.

Index

Order Form

_____ **"The Answer is NO": Saying it and sticking to it - $12.95**

_____ **Win the Whining War & Other Skirmishes - $12.95**
This is a step-by-step guide to increasing cooperation and reducing conflict
with children 2-12 years old. These effective techniques will help you
eliminate whining, tantraums, dawdling, bad language, teasing,
complaining, and all the annoying behavior that drives you crazy. The
author, Cynthia Whitham, is staff therapist at the renowned UCLA Parent
Training Program.

_____ **Survival Tips for Working Moms - $10.95**
This book offers hundreds of real solutions that real working moms use
every day. From packing school lunches to supervising homework, from
getting the kids to do chores to finding after school care, from getting out the
door in the morning to making adult time without the kids, author Linda
Goodman Pillsbury offers concrete suggestions for making life easier. The
book is full of examples of how the tips work in real families.

Please add $3.50 shipping for first book, .50 for each additional
book. California residents add sales tax (and indicate which county
you are in)

Name: _____

Address: _____

_____

Phone:(____)_____   Total Enclosed: $_____

Send to: Perspective Publishing, Inc.
            50 S. DeLacey Ave. #201
            Pasadena, CA 91105

or

ORDER TOLL FREE 1-800-992-6657